# NO BOUNDARIES

## 25 WOMEN EXPLORERS AND SCIENTISTS
## SHARE ADVENTURES, INSPIRATION, AND ADVICE

Clare Fieseler and Gabby Salazar

NATIONAL
GEOGRAPHIC

WASHINGTON, D.C.

# TABLE OF CONTENTS

GABBY SALAZAR (LEFT), CLARE FIESELER (CENTER), AND MOREANGELS MBIZAH (RIGHT) POSE WITH NATIONAL GEOGRAPHIC SOCIETY'S FLAG.

# INTRODUCTION

**S**tanding outside our tents on the savanna, we heard elephants in the distance. Stars twinkled brightly above, and the moon cast a dim glow across the landscape below. We were camping out in Hwange National Park, Zimbabwe, with Dr. Moreangels Mbizah, one of the brave scientists featured in this book.

We had traveled together to Zimbabwe from our homes in the United States to make a short film about Moreangels—her research tracking lions and the challenges she'd faced as a woman in science. National Geographic had funded our trip so we could tell her story, and the stories of other women pushing boundaries in challenging situations around the globe. Our desire to tell these stories led us to Zimbabwe and, also, to writing this book.

Inside these pages, you'll encounter women who've done, and are still doing, incredible things. You'll read about their careers, read their words of wisdom, and learn about the awesome animals, places, and cultures they've encountered.

The women in this book have traveled the world to protect animals, tell stories, preserve history, complete incredible athletic feats—and so much more. And yet, we've rarely seen media showing women like these in the field, getting dirty, confronting biases, and changing the world.

Ultimately, we created this book because it's a book we wish we had when we were growing up. We chose to write about women who inspired us—women whose grit and ingenuity led them to do great things, whether in their backyards or on Mars. Each woman's story tells of a different path, a certain struggle, or a unique way of getting started. The women on these pages aren't from another century. They are on the front lines of science and exploration today.

We hope these stories show you that there is no one path to changing the world and doing what matters. We hope they show you that there is no one way that a scientist should look, or one place that an explorer should come from. We hope you find inspiration in them, just as we do.

Gabby and Clare
National Geographic Explorers

# DOMINIQUE GONÇALVES

## ECOLOGIST

An ecologist studies and monitors all aspects of life in an ecosystem, including numbers of living things, life cycles, and animal behavior.

The elephants of Gorongosa National Park in Mozambique (a country in southeastern Africa) were in danger of being wiped out completely. For 15 years, a devastating civil war tore the country apart. During that time, soldiers sold the elephants' ivory tusks to buy weapons, and they hunted them to have something to eat. By the end of the war, in 1992, more than 90 percent of the park's large mammals had been killed and only 100 elephants remained. Ecologist Dominique Gonçalves is among the young scientists determined to help restore and conserve the park and its animal inhabitants.

Dominique was born in the city of Beira, Mozambique, just as the civil war was ending. "I was lucky to be born in the year of peace and to have a peaceful childhood," she says. That peaceful childhood included a deep love and appreciation for science—biology in particular.

In college, Dominique narrowed her focus to ecology and conservation, specializing in medium and large animals. Then, toward the end of her undergraduate program, she learned that a new science lab had just opened at Gorongosa. Dominique had read about the work being done to restore the wildlife in the park, and she wanted to be part of that effort.

Even though she didn't know of any available job openings, Dominique wanted to make sure the people working at the park knew she was interested. So she sent an email to the lab. "I asked them if they had any internships," Dominique says, "and I told them I didn't want any money, I just wanted to be there."

The answer was no. They said the lab was still too new, and they weren't yet offering internships. But three days later, Dominique got an email from the director of Scientific Services. She laughs remembering their meeting: "I think he was just interested in finding out, *Who is this girl who really wants to come here?*"

Taking the initiative to send that first email changed the course of Dominique's whole life. It took more than a year, but finally she was called about an opening at the park.

Dominique's first encounter with elephants at Gorongosa was pretty spectacular. The elephants weren't bathing in a stream or calmly walking in a field. No—the very first time she saw them in the park, they were charging toward her and a group of other scientists. "It was a breathtaking experience," she says. "There in the wild, you really realize how majestic and powerful they are."

To study the elephants, Dominique tracks and photographs them, and sometimes tags them with GPS satellite collars. She also monitors their movements, growth, health, and behavior. Sometimes the elephants are briefly sedated so that she and other scientists can quickly collect samples (like blood and saliva) for further testing.

Dominique experienced one particularly powerful experience during her training. She and her mentor, an elephant researcher named Joyce Poole, had spotted a young elephant calf with an injured leg. They set out to find the calf again, in hopes of bringing him to the veterinarian. During the search, they encountered an agitated adult female

> ❝ There in the wild, you really realize how majestic and powerful elephants are. ❞

elephant. As soon as she saw them, the elephant began charging in all directions and behaving very strangely. She knocked down two trees. Then she took a branch from one of them and used it to hit herself on the back. It was clear that the elephant was very stressed, but Dominique couldn't understand why.

Then, from out of the bushes, the injured calf they'd seen earlier suddenly appeared. It walked over to the female elephant—who must have been its mother! "I realized, this poor mother was trying to protect her injured baby," Dominique says. "You can read about it in books, but for me—only when I saw that situation did I really understand that each elephant is an individual, with complex relationships and emotions, including empathy."

While Dominique was in training, her trips in the field were always with other people, including someone who would drive the jeep. With experienced guides and colleagues, she always felt safe. But eventually, Dominique began going out on these trips alone. She now had to drive, make observations, and do everything herself. It was a lot of responsibility, and at times, she wondered if she'd be able to do it all.

One day, not long after setting off on her own, Dominique was tasked with showing a film crew around the park. They wanted to film elephants going about their daily lives. She located a group of five bull elephants and parked the jeep a safe distance away. One of the elephants, whose name was Aloisio, started to move toward them, coming up behind the jeep—and he got really close. "My heart was pounding," she says. "I knew if Joyce were there, she'd have been taking pictures. But I couldn't move!"

Frozen, she stayed perfectly still, trying not to even breathe. When someone in the car said, "Oh my gosh!" Dominique quickly shushed them. This elephant was huge. And if things went wrong, it could mean big trouble. Finally, when she mustered the courage to turn and look at Aloisio, he was so close that Dominique could see her own face reflected in his eye. The elephant seemed very curious, not upset, and he even bent his head as if trying to get a better look at Dominique. "I wondered if he could hear my heart beating very fast," she says. But then, after a quiet, peaceful moment, he lifted his head, looked around, and slowly led the other elephants away to a nearby lagoon.

"From then on, I felt like I could do this," she says. "If he saw me and decided he should not harm me, maybe I could really do some work with him. I felt connected. It's not every day you see your own reflection in the eye of an elephant."

Today, thanks to the Gorongosa Restoration Project, more than 650 elephants live in the park, and that number is on the rise. Dominique is particularly interested in studying conflicts between humans and elephants and trying to foster understanding between the two groups so that they can peacefully coexist. "Humans live very close to areas where wildlife lives," Dominique says, "which means we are often competing for resources, like water, space, and food." Sometimes when humans and elephants clash (like when elephants eat farmers' crops), one or both can get hurt. Dominique wants to help prevent these clashes by studying this problem and identifying possible solutions. These include working with community members to adjust their perceptions of elephants, as well as identifying particularly sensitive areas and situations where these conflicts might occur.

Success in restoring a park like Gorongosa depends on the support of the community around it. That's why Dominique works to help people and elephants learn more about each other—so that the park, the animals, and the community can thrive together, long into the future.

## INSPIRATION STATION
### Dominique's Advice for Aspiring Scientists

"If you see an opportunity, take it. But even if there is no opportunity—make one. Also, be persistent. My first assignment in the field was just to walk and collect data, but the rangers leading the trip were skeptical, thinking, *She won't be able to walk 10 kilometers [6 miles] a day.* And you know what, we actually ended up walking 30 kilometers [19 miles] a day! My supervisor was so proud. If you want to do something, the important thing is not to quit! You can do it."

## DOMINIQUE'S MUST-HAVE

Three big things: binoculars, a backpack, and a water bottle. The reason I need a backpack is because I'm very short and the driver's seat in the Jeep doesn't move forward," Dominique says. "So for my legs to reach the pedals, I wear my backpack when I drive."

# CREATE A WILDLIFE HABITAT
# IN YOUR OWN
# BACKYARD

Just like at Gorongosa, animal populations all around the world are impacted by human activity. And it doesn't take something as tragic (or violent) as a civil war to endanger wildlife. In fact, all it takes is for humans to encroach, or intrude, onto land where wild animals live. The good thing is that you can make a difference. Your own backyard can become a safe place for animals that live in your neighborhood, or that are just passing through, to rest, eat, breed, and sleep.

**Try it for yourself! All you need is the following:**

## FOOD

Provide a variety of food sources. These can be things like bird feeders and hummingbird feeders, or naturally occurring food sources like berries, seeds, pollen, and nectar. Be sure to grow flowers and plants that are native to your area, so that the birds, butterflies, bees, small critters, and other animals will be familiar with them.

Different plants and types of food attract different animals. What kind of animals would you like to attract to your backyard?

# WATER

Animals need water to drink and bathe, and some need it to breed. If you live near a body of water, then you're all set. But if you don't, you can find a container, put some rocks or pebbles at the bottom, and fill it with water. Try not to use anything that's super slippery—the animals will need to get a secure hold to be able to lean in to have a drink.

Backyard wildlife habitats can attract all sorts of animals, like birds, butterflies, bees, and more!

# SHELTER

Animals sometimes need a place to get out of the open, hide from predators, or seek refuge from bad weather. This could be a pile of logs or rocks, brush, a dead tree stump, or even a birdhouse or pond.

# A PLACE FOR LITTLE ONES

Some kinds of shelter can help animals safely care for their young—such as birdhouses, trees, nesting boxes, or dense shrubs.

# GO GREEN!

Maintain your wildlife habitat in an environmentally friendly way by doing your best to conserve water and soil, avoid using chemical pesticides and fertilizers, and remove any invasive, non-native species.

# WASFIA
## NAZREEN

### MOUNTAINEER AND ACTIVIST

A mountaineer is a person who climbs mountains for sport. Mountaineering requires skills in hiking, climbing, skiing, camping, and outdoor safety. An activist uses direct actions and communication to inspire political or social change.

**WASFIA ENJOYS THE SUN WHILE RESTING AT A MOUNT EVEREST BASE CAMP.**

The Seven Summits

At the base of Denali, in Alaska, U.S.A., Wasfia Nazreen awoke to the peaceful sound of water boiling. It was summer in the Arctic, and even at night the icy landscape glowed silvery in the midnight sun. First thing every morning, Wasfia and her climbing partner dug up clean chunks of ice, fired up the camp stove, and melted the ice to fill their water bottles. Then they began another long day's trek as part of their perilous, 16-mile (26-km) climb to the summit, or highest point, of the highest mountain in North America. To this day, says Wasfia, "Even when I am back home in Bangladesh, when I hear the sound of water boiling, it is very calming, and it takes me back to the mountains."

Wasfia hadn't always been a mountaineer. Where she grew up in South Asia, there were rolling hills—not massive, snowcapped mountains. But when she moved to northern India in college she was among proper mountains. She was working as a journalist and social worker, helping refugees from Tibet who lived in the foothills of the Himalaya.

Through her work, she traveled throughout the region, to places like Tibet, Bhutan, and Nepal. Many of her colleagues were local mountaineers, and while Wasfia hadn't set out to learn how to become a mountain climber, that's exactly what happened over time. "It was a lifestyle I just naturally picked up," she says.

Wasfia soon realized she acclimated well to high altitudes. In places higher than 8,000 feet (2,400 m) above sea level, where there are low levels of oxygen, some people experience a number of unpleasant symptoms, including headache, nausea, and vomiting. Thankfully, Wasfia did not. She began trying some high-altitude treks in the Himalaya, and with the help of a friend who became her climbing guru, she learned the skills she needed to become a great mountaineer.

Today, Wasfia is one of only a few hundred people in the world (and, so far, the only person from the relatively flat, often flooded country of Bangladesh) to ever climb the Seven Summits—the highest mountains on each of Earth's seven continents. For her, the most difficult climb was to the peak of Denali, in Alaska. It wasn't the highest mountain—both Mount Everest in Nepal and Cerro Aconcagua in Argentina are higher—but it was the most personally challenging. And because of that, it was also the most fulfilling. "Unlike the more familiar Everest," Wasfia says, "Denali took me three tries!" The first time, she and her climbing partner had to wait out some bad weather at Camp 14—a resting place at an elevation of 14,000 feet (4,300 m). If the weather weren't bad enough, Wasfia also became terribly ill.

"I accidentally built my toilet too close to my kitchen," she says, referring to the igloo-style shelters they made along the way. "I ended up with a bad case of diarrhea." Still feeling sick after four days, she realized that even if they did make it to the summit, she wouldn't be healthy enough to get back down the mountain safely. It had taken her eight months to raise the funds she needed to attempt Denali, and when she realized it wasn't going to happen, she was devastated. She didn't know if she'd ever be able to come back and try again.

But she did. And the second time didn't go as planned either. She and her partner were at the last stop before the summit when they got caught in a storm. Snow and icy winds blew in and persisted for two weeks. "Our food ran out, and we were told by rangers to go down," Wasfia says. "But we were stuck. There was no way to get down in that intense weather."

While waiting for the winds to die down, Wasfia dashed outside her tent to go to the bathroom. She took off her gloves for just a split second, and later that night she realized she'd gotten frostbite on one of her fingers. The pain soon became excruciating. She could see the summit—she was less than 3,000 feet (900 m) from it, but she knew she had to begin her climb down. It took six surgeries to save her finger, and recovery was slow. For more than a year, if Wasfia was in cold or snowy places, she would experience terrible pain.

When she finally recovered, she knew she had to try a third time. Even when some concerned friends and family were discouraging her from trying again, she was determined. "I was committed to completing the Seven Summits," she says. Even more, she could see the positive effect her journey was having on young girls and others in Bangladesh, and that spurred her on. Regular people were watching Wasfia's journey and changing their ideas about what women could and should do. They were so inspired by her journey they often helped her any way they could. "I've had women give me their

gold wedding jewelry to help raise funds, and I've had fathers walk all the way from north of Bangladesh to bring their daughters to meet me and tell me that I inspired them."

Finally reaching that last ridge on the way to the Denali summit is a moment she will always remember. "It was a very beautiful, sunny summit," she says. "I was so overwhelmed with emotions, and I just felt really grateful. Reaching the summit meant way more to me than if I had climbed it in one go. Before those three attempts, I had climbed five of the Seven Summits, back to back. The fact that I got frostbite was the universe's way of telling me to slow down, to soak it all in, to take in the journey."

When Wasfia reached the top of Puncak Jaya (Mount Carstensz), a year after Denali, she became the first Bangladeshi—man or woman—to ever complete the Seven Summits. All across the country, girls and young women had been excitedly following her progress on social media. Bangladeshi men and boys were inspired by her courage as well.

Wasfia's climbs came at a meaningful time for her country. And that was no accident. While Wasfia was preparing and climbing the Seven Summits, Bangladesh was celebrating the 40th anniversary of its independence.

In those 40 years, there had been a lot of progress for women in Bangladesh—women now have more freedom and greater opportunities to get an education than before. Wasfia wanted to celebrate that.

Together with some of her supporters, Wasfia formed the Ösel Foundation, where girls and youth in difficult situations can learn mindfulness and experience outdoor activities. "We want to encourage them to discover themselves, to be able to make their own decisions, and to not have others choose their life paths for them," she says. For Wasfia, who has seen the awesome beauty of the world from seven of its highest peaks, her greatest goal now is to empower girls and women to reach for new heights of their own.

> **66**
> Reaching the summit meant way more to me than if I had climbed it in one go.
> **99**

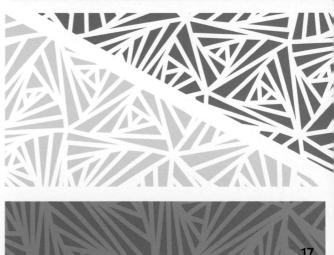

WASFIA TRAINS ON A FROZEN RIVER IN BRITISH COLUMBIA, CANADA, HAULING DISCARDED TIRES FROM A NEARBY DUMP.

Preparing to become a mountaineer takes a lot of training. You need to do plenty of cardiovascular exercise (like running, biking, and climbing) as well as weight training. Plus, your body needs to get used to being at high altitudes.

## WASFIA'S MUST-HAVE

A tiny protective amulet and cord from her teacher. On each of her Seven Summit treks, Wasfia brought an amulet given by the Dalai Lama—the spiritual leader of Tibet—for protection while traversing sacred mountains.

## INSPIRATION STATION
### Wasfia's Advice for Aspiring Adventurers

"The thing to realize is that no matter what we do, there will be someone who has a problem with our decisions. It's very important that we focus on our path and know that anything is possible if we put our mind into it. It takes a lot of effort to stick to your dreams when there are many people trying to tell you what to do. This is not just a problem for girls in Bangladesh, but all over the world. So, if you have a dream, believe that it is truly possible, and go for it!"

# PEAK PERFORMANCE
## MAPPING THE SEVEN SUMMITS

The famed Seven Summits are the highest peaks on each of the seven continents. Summiting them, which means making it all the way to the top, is a dream for many climbers. Depending on which expert you ask, though, there are slightly different versions of the Seven Summits. These are the summits Wasfia climbed.

### EVEREST
**Asia (at the border between Nepal and China)**
**29,032 FEET
(8,849 METERS)**

# CERRO ACONCAGUA
**South America**
**Mendoza Province, Argentina**
**22,838 FEET (6,961 METERS)**

# DENALI
**North America, Alaska, U.S.A.**
**20,322 FEET (6,194 METERS)**

# KILIMANJARO
**Africa, Tanzania**
**19,341 FEET (5,895 METERS)**

# ELBRUS
**Europe, Southern Russia**
**(near the border with Georgia)**
**18,510 FEET (5,642 METERS)**

# MOUNT VINSON
**Antarctica**
**16,050 FEET (4,892 METERS)**

# PUNCAK JAYA
**(MOUNT CARSTENSZ)**
**Australasia, Indonesia**
**16,024 FEET (4,884 METERS)**

# AUBREY
# ROBERTS

Svalbard
archipelago,
Norway

## PALEONTOLOGIST

Paleontologists find and study
fossils, and they use these fossils
to discover and tell us more
about the history of life on Earth.

It was August in the Arctic, a time of year when the sun never sets. The snow on the mountainside was melting, and the ground underfoot felt squishy.

"It's usually not freezing," Dr. Aubrey Roberts says, describing her summer fieldwork in Svalbard, a Norwegian archipelago in the Arctic Ocean. "But imagine you're out camping for two weeks, and you don't ever feel warm. You get wet and muddy, digging for fossils all day, and you never really get dry. Then the wind starts blowing! I remember having five different layers on, and I still felt chilled to the bone."

In spite of the cold, Aubrey knew since her first trip to Svalbard that this is exactly what she wanted to do. "When I'm there," she says, "I feel like I never want to leave." The vast, nearly treeless landscape is a paleontologist's dream—with exposed rock layers full of fossils no one has ever seen before.

Aubrey fell in love with dinosaurs when she was just three years old. "The first words I could say, apart from 'Mum' and 'Dad,' were awesome dinosaur names, like *Parasaurolophus, Velociraptor,* and *Stegosaurus*," she says. When she started college, she didn't realize it was even possible to become a paleontologist. She majored in biology at the University of Oslo, in Norway. While her professors there pointed her in the right direction, it was Aubrey's decision to actively seek out a new opportunity that changed her life.

After hearing a lecture about the fossils of Svalbard, a chain of islands in the Arctic Ocean, Aubrey sent the professor an email and asked him if he needed another student to help with his upcoming project. He said yes! Aubrey soon became a member of the project's Spitsbergen Mesozoic Research Group. For two weeks every summer, the team travels to the far north to look for and excavate the fossil remains of marine reptiles that lived during the time of the dinosaurs.

"There aren't many people up there," Aubrey says, "but there are polar bears, arctic foxes, and reindeer. Before we went, the team was trained on how to stay safe in what can, at times, be a very dangerous environment."

As soon as they arrived, they set up a trip wire around the whole area where they would be camping. It was their alarm system, which would go off if a polar bear came too close. All of their food was stored in one special tent, apart from the others. "In our sleeping tents, we tried to avoid having anything that smelled—even toothpaste," Aubrey says, "because the bears are very curious and will want to check out anything that smells interesting."

Once camp was set up, the team began their search for any clues that there could be fossils nearby. Aubrey still remembers the team's excitement after one particularly special find. First, they spotted a few fossilized bones poking out of the ground, and right away they could see that the bones were well preserved. There was a long string of neck bones that seemed to snake straight into the mountainside. That long neck could belong to only one animal—a plesiosaur. In the time of dinosaurs, the plesiosaur was a huge marine reptile. Its neck could easily stretch for more than six feet (2 m)! Aubrey and her team wondered if, at the end of that neck—maybe, just maybe—there could be a skull hiding in the mountain.

"Our team had never found a plesiosaur skull before," Aubrey says. "The skulls are tiny and

> **I remember having five different layers on, and I still felt chilled to the bone.**

fragile, so they're very rare. But we were so excited—we really wanted to find it there." The only way to do that was to remove a lot of rock—carefully uncovering the neck bones, or vertebrae, one by one. But when they finally got to the end, there was no skull.

"We just sat there in utter despair, in the muddy puddle that was our excavation site," Aubrey says. They decided to slog back down the mountain and have a rest. But one of the professors wasn't ready to throw in the towel. He stayed and he kept brushing away more dirt and more rock, and within minutes, just a few inches from where they'd uncovered the neck, there it was—a complete skull!

It wasn't until Aubrey and her team were all back at camp that they had time to sit back and take in how important their discovery was. "This was the only plesiosaur we'd ever found with its skull so well preserved," Aubrey says. "And not only that—it looked like it might be a completely new type of plesiosaur!"

After they'd excavated the skull and the other bones of the skeleton, they needed to transport them to the museum in Oslo. To protect the delicate fossils, they encased them in plaster jackets. Then they had the heavy jackets airlifted by helicopter to the largest port town in Svalbard, where they could be shipped to the museum. At the museum, people who were trained to prepare the fossils carefully opened the jackets and began the time-consuming task of removing all the excess rock and dirt, and gluing any broken bones back together. Then the scientific research could begin.

While the whole team believed that the plesiosaur they'd discovered was a species new to science, they had to find out for sure. Aubrey took photos of all the bones and traveled to museums around the world to compare plesiosaur specimens. After many observations and measurements, the team's suspicions were confirmed—it was a new species!

To announce this exciting news to the world, Aubrey wrote a paper about the new plesiosaur, which helped her complete her Ph.D., and published it in a science journal. "It took seven years from excavation to publication," Aubrey says, "but the whole process has been very exciting." Today, because of her and her team's hard work, the world has learned something new about plesiosaurs, and one more detail has been revealed about the history of life on Earth.

## STRAIGHT FROM THE SCIENTIST

### Are there any female paleontologists from history who have inspired you?

"As someone who has worked so much on marine reptiles, I have to say—Mary Anning. She lived during the early 1800s, the Victorian era, and she really did her best in what were very difficult times for women in science. She excavated the world's first ichthyosaur and the first plesiosaur. She prepared all the specimens and illustrated them for scientific papers that were published by men."

Plesiosaurs went extinct 66 million years ago, at the end of the Cretaceous period.

## WHAT'S IN A NAME?

When Aubrey and a fellow student were excavating their plesiosaur skeleton, they had a song by pop star Britney Spears running through their heads, so they nicknamed the specimen "Britney." Important new fossils get assigned specimen numbers, such as Britney's: PMO 224.248. These numbers get put on the fossil and in the museum's database, so anyone can look up where, when, and by whom the specimens were found. But fun field names are essential, too. They're much easier for paleontologists to remember when they're out working in the field. Of course, now Britney's species has the official, scientific name of *Ophthalmothule cryostea*.

## AUBREY'S MUST-HAVE

A pillow! When braving extreme conditions for days and nights on end, bringing a few creature comforts from home can be a game changer. "The first year I went out in the field, I did not have a pillow with me, and I also had a thin sleeping bag," Aubrey says. "I was very cold and not very happy."

The largest plesiosaur could grow to more than 40 feet (12 m) long. That's about as long as six queen-size beds lined up end to end!

## INSPIRATION STATION
### Aubrey's Advice for Aspiring Paleontologists

"Don't give up! Follow your passion. Even if the road seems difficult and winding—go for it, because it is an amazing job to have. I wish for every aspiring paleontologist to experience being out in the field—wherever you can."

## AUBREY'S READING REC

*Raptor Red* by Robert Bakker. It's a novel that follows the life of a *Utahraptor* (a predatory dinosaur the size of a grizzly bear)—from its birth until its death. "It was an amazing, brilliant book," Aubrey says. "It really swept me away into the Cretaceous period and allowed me to imagine what it must have been like to be a dinosaur."

# THE DIRT

A lot of careful work goes into removing a huge fossil from the ground—and keeping it in great condition! Check out how Aubrey and her team get the job done.

**1** Uncover all the bones so that you know exactly how far they extend.

**2** Carefully dig a trench around the specimen. If you have a really big specimen, you may need to trench around separate parts of the skeleton, so you'll end up with a few chunks that are smaller and more manageable.

**3** Cover the bones in wet toilet paper (thick high-quality stuff works best).

**4** Cut long strips of burlap and soak them in plaster. Then lay the plaster-soaked strips over the layer of toilet paper until your specimen is completely covered.

**5** Plaster iron rods into the top of the plaster jacket to support it.

# ON DIGS

**6** Take a short break to let the plaster dry. You now have your specimen half-encased in a hard plaster jacket. Dig underneath the plaster jacket all around until it is sitting on a small pedestal of rock. (It'll look like a mushroom shape!)

**7** Hammer giant, custom-made steel stakes under the specimen, to crack the pedestal of rock underneath.

**8** Tie rope around the ends of the stakes and across the jacket and then use the stakes on one side as levers to carefully flip the jacket over. This takes a lot of muscle power!

**9** Trim down some of the rock on the underside of the jacket and cover that in toilet paper and plaster strips, too, so that you have a closed plaster jacket (like a smooth white pod) around the specimen.

**10** Strap the jacket onto a wooden platform. It can then be airlifted by helicopter to a place where it can be shipped by boat or truck to a museum.

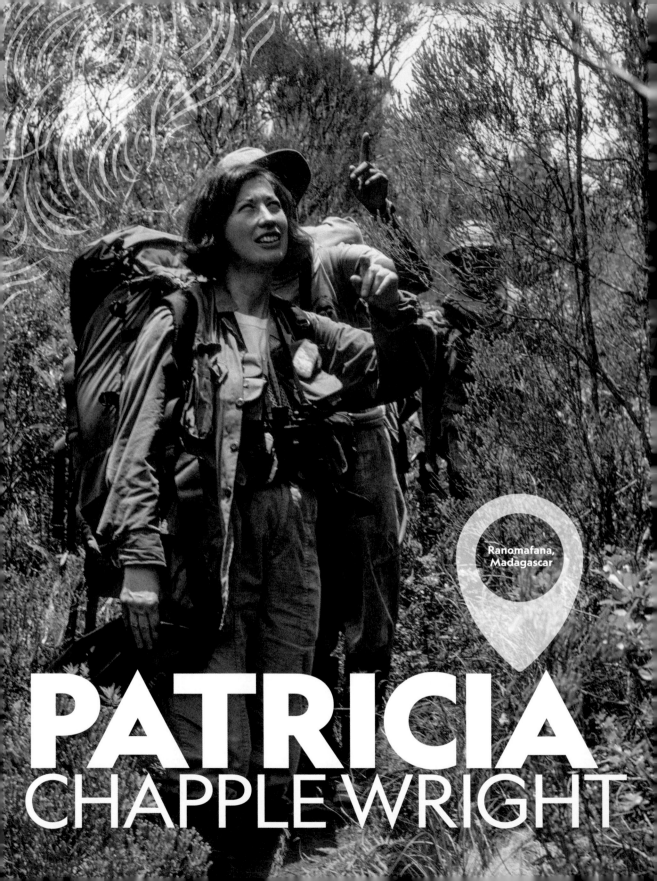

Ranomafana, Madagascar

# PATRICIA
## CHAPPLE WRIGHT

A primatologist is a type of zoologist who studies primates—a group of mammals that includes lemurs, monkeys, apes, and humans. A conservationist is a person who works to preserve and protect wildlife and the environment.

Dr. Patricia Wright has always loved animals. As a little girl growing up on her family's farm, she would sit outside and watch the birds. When it was time to choose a career path, Patricia says, "While I knew that I loved animals, I had no idea that working with animals was a job option." She majored in biology, but once she graduated, she set her interest in animals aside.

Her first job, in the 1970s, was as a social worker in New York City, working to help people who were struggling financially to get a better education and find jobs. It was important work, but something inside of her couldn't let go of the feeling that she wanted to work with animals. She had long had a fascination with the Amazon rainforest, and that led her to focus on some of its most fascinating inhabitants—primates.

"It isn't really that I decided as much as it was my heart that decided," Patricia says. "I wanted to study these animals and find out everything I could about them." So, she began working on a Ph.D. in primatology at the City University of New York, focusing specifically on the owl monkey. By the time she'd completed her doctorate, she was one of only very few scientists who had observed and studied this elusive animal—the world's only nocturnal monkey—in the wild.

> **"**
> I had no idea that working with animals was a job option.
> **"**

In 1986, after she finished graduate school, the director of the Primate Center at Duke University asked her if she'd be interested in looking for another nocturnal animal—the greater bamboo lemur. She'd loved watching the colony of lemurs at Duke. And, she says, "I found out that lemurs are matriarchal, which means females lead the group—that intrigued me."

So, she agreed to help. She'd never been to Madagascar, and she was up for the adventure. The trouble was, no one had seen this species in the wild in more than 50 years. No one was even sure if it still existed. It would be like looking for a needle in a haystack.

She knew that greater bamboo lemurs ate bamboo stalks, so she and her team of American and Malagasy researchers started by exploring areas where bamboo grew, and where people had reported seeing the lemurs in the past. They combed through the woods, looking for signs—a chewed bamboo stalk on the forest floor, or a pile of lemur poop. Week after frustrating week, they found nothing. Exhausted, they took some time to go to the hot springs near the town of Ranomafana for a hot bath and a little rest. The forest near there looked interesting, so they decided to do some exploring there before they left. And it was there, one cold, foggy morning, while Patricia and a teammate were out walking, that they spotted it.

"We were so excited," says Patricia. "The animal made a noise like a motor starting up. It stared at us for a minute or two, and then it leapt away." They'd finally seen a greater bamboo lemur!

Or so they thought.

Not long after that encounter, says Patricia, "We found an actual greater bamboo lemur in the same forest, and it looked very different." It was gray, and it ate thick stalks of bamboo. The first lemur had been golden in color, and it ate the tender young bamboo shoots that came out of the ground. Amazingly, the lemur they saw that misty morning was a new species—one that had never before been described by science. Patricia named it the golden bamboo lemur. "'Golden' is a good name for it," Patricia says, "because of its beautiful color and because, like gold, it really is a treasure of the rainforest."

Alas, as soon as Patricia realized she'd discovered a new lemur, she also realized, with horror, that a timber company was hard at work, cutting down the very trees the lemurs needed to live. She worried that golden bamboo lemurs would go extinct before she even had a chance to study them. At that moment, she knew that to save these lemurs she'd have to step beyond her role as a scientist and act as a conservationist, too. At first it felt like too much to take on. But Patricia persisted. She spoke with officials at Madagascar's Department of Water and Forest and tried to persuade them to create a new national park that would encompass the Ranomafana rainforest, where the golden bamboo lemurs and greater bamboo lemurs lived.

While they said that they would love to create a national park, it wasn't that simple. Creating one would require millions of dollars, which they did not have. At the time, Patricia had no idea how to raise that kind of money, but she was determined to help. She and her team began raising the funds, and much to their surprise, they did it! Ranomafana National Park was officially established in 1991. Today, you can visit the park and see the golden bamboo lemurs and the greater bamboo lemurs, as well as 10 other lemur species. Patricia and her graduate students continue to study the lemurs there, and she is thrilled to report that their numbers are rising.

"Even though these animals are still critically endangered," she says, "they're much less endangered than they were a decade or two ago." In fact, today there are three times as many golden bamboo lemurs in the park as there were when her team began. "I don't think I ever had confidence that these things could be done. But I realized that it was the right thing to do, so I wanted to try. If you don't try, you don't succeed. But, if you do try, there's at least hope that you can." And this time, Patricia and her team did!

Most primates don't have sharp claws like cats, dogs, or birds do. Instead, they have flattened nails.

## INSPIRATION STATION
### Patricia's Advice for Aspiring Scientists

"Don't forget that there are a lot of things to discover out there. It's extremely important to study hard, get as much knowledge as you can, and go out there and explore. There will be people who tell you that you can't do this or you can't do that. They are just trying to be practical. They don't mean any harm, but sometimes you just have to be insistent about what it is you really want to do. I don't think it's ever easy—but it is so worth it."

## PATRICIA'S MUST-HAVE

Binoculars! They are an essential tool for wild-life watchers. They'll help you get a close-up look, without actually getting too close and bothering the animals you want to observe.

The fossa is Madagascar's biggest carnivore—and the lemur's biggest preda-tor. It looks a little like a mountain lion, but it's not a cat. It's actually more closely related to the mongoose!

# ISLAND OF LEMURS

Lemurs' distant ancestors evolved on the continent of Africa, more than 50 million years ago. During violent rainstorms, a few of them were swept out across the ocean on rafts of tangled branches and leaves. Those lucky enough to land on the coast of Madagascar found an island paradise with few competi-tors. Over the course of millions of years, the lemurs on the African continent went extinct, but the migrant lemurs thrived. Over time, many different species evolved, in different shapes and sizes, and with a variety of unique behaviors.

Since then, life has gotten tougher and tougher for lemurs. Because of habitat loss caused by human activity, as well as hunting, lemurs have become endangered. Today, about 90 percent of the lemurs' habitat is gone, and in spite of the best efforts of conservationists, the lemurs remain in danger of going extinct.

29

# Madagascar's
## Unique Wildlife

Africa
Atlantic Ocean
MADAGASCAR
Europe
Asia
Indian Ocean

TANZANIA
ZAMBIA
MALAWI
MOZAMBIQUE
ZIMBABWE
SOUTH AFRICA
ESWATINI
LESOTHO
COMOROS
SEYCHELLES
INDIAN OCEAN
MADAGASCAR
MAURITIUS
INDIAN OCEAN

Two hundred million years ago, the island of Madagascar slowly began to split apart from the continent of Africa. Then, about 80 million years ago, the landmass that would become present-day India tore away from Madagascar and began its long, slow drift to the northeast. With that, Madagascar became completely isolated. And, because of its remote location, over 80 percent of the more than 200,000 species that live there can be found nowhere else on Earth. That includes the approximately 100 species of lemurs that call Madagascar home. Take a look at some of these eye-popping, tree-hopping primates.

**RING-TAILED LEMUR**

Today, the indri is the island's largest lemur, growing to about 28 inches (71 cm) long and weighing between 13 and 21 pounds (6–9.5 kg).

**INDRI (OR BABAKOTO)**

**RED RUFFED LEMUR**

With their distinctive tails and bold facial markings, ring-tailed lemurs are the iconic animal of Madagascar.

VERREAUX'S SIFAKA

BLACK AND WHITE RUFFED LEMUR

AYE-AYE

The golden bamboo lemur lives in the rainforest and eats the young leaves and new shoots of bamboo.

ANKARANA SPORTIVE LEMUR

The Ankarana sportive lemur spends most of its day sleeping in a leafy branch or hollow of a tree. At night, this lemur comes to life, searching for tasty leaves and small flowers to eat.

GOLDEN BAMBOO LEMUR

31

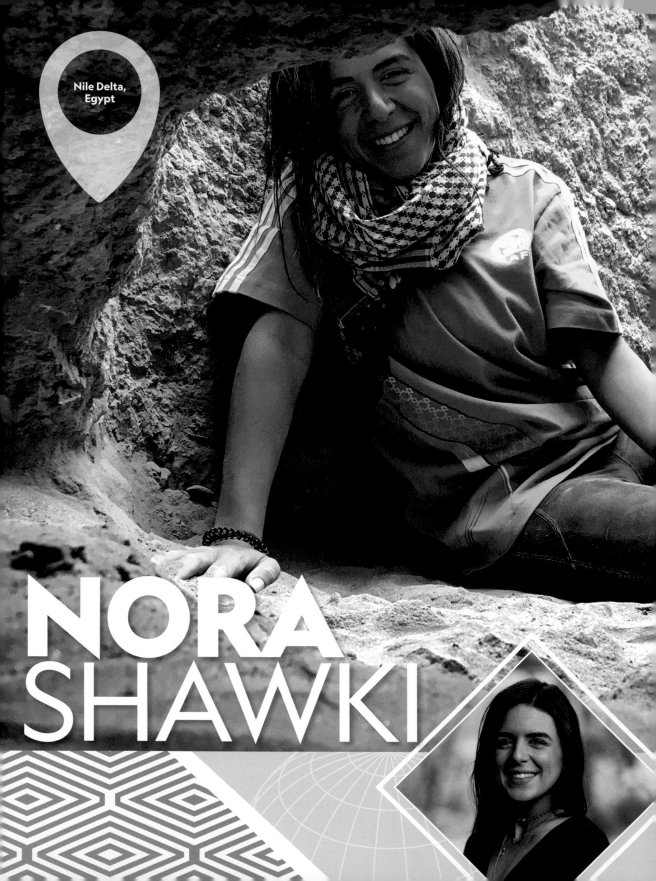

# NORA
# SHAWKI

## ARCHAEOLOGIST

An archaeologist uncovers,
records, and studies the physical
objects left behind in areas where
humans once lived, to find clues
about what their lives were like.

W hen she was nine years old, in school in Egypt, Nora Shawki saw a film that she'll never forget. It was a reenactment of the British archaeologist Howard Carter discovering the tomb of the young pharaoh Tutankhamun, or "King Tut," in Egypt's Valley of the Kings. "They'd just discovered the tomb, and Carter was entering the burial chamber for the first time ever," Nora says, describing her favorite scene. "He made a little hole in the doorway. Then, he held up his candle to the hole and peered in. One of the workmen asked, 'What do you see?' As his candle lit up the gold and ebony treasures within, all Carter said was, 'Wonderful things.' From that moment—I was sold! I knew exactly what I wanted to do with my life."

Once she was in college, choosing which subject to major in was easy—it would, of course, be archaeology. After graduating, she went on to earn a master's degree, and while the treasures of royal Egyptians continued to fascinate her, she became even more fascinated by the lives of ordinary people. She wondered: *Where did they live? What did they eat? How did they worship? What were their houses and villages like?* She'd gotten the education she needed to begin answering some of these questions. But the road to actually becoming an archaeologist, she admits, was not as easy as she had expected.

She focused her attention on the Nile Delta in northern Egypt, where the Nile River flows into the Mediterranean Sea. The Nile provides water and enriches the soil, and people have lived and farmed in this area for thousands of years. She began looking closely at settlements that existed right before the end of the Egyptian Empire, between 600 and 334 B.C. And she had chosen some possible sites she wanted to study. "I applied to eight or nine different organizations in a row, hoping to get the opportunity to join a study," Nora says. After getting rejection letters from all but one of the organizations, she had just about given up hope. Her last application was to National Geographic, to lead a dig of her own. This was her "dream project," but the one she thought she was most unlikely to get. Much to her surprise, the organization accepted her application, and she received a grant, or money for her project. All she had to do was get the permit necessary to dig at the site she wanted, and the grant would provide the funding.

"All of those rejection letters made this one acceptance so much sweeter," Nora says. The grant was for a site in the delta called Tell Zuwelen. Royal tombs had been discovered near this site, and Nora thought this may have been the settlement where the people who built those tombs actually lived. But getting the permit to dig there turned out to be even harder than getting the funding.

"I discovered there's a lot of paperwork—a lot of applications to fill out—before you can work in the field. I spent a year and a half fighting to get that permit from Egypt's Ministry of Antiquities."

When the ministry finally approved her permit, Nora went to the site to begin her survey. She spoke with the leader of the village, and he told her he was the one who'd been holding up her permit for so long. "He said he knew exactly who I was, and that he didn't want anyone to excavate at this site," Nora says. She spoke with some of the villagers, who supported her work, but even they said, "You can try to dig here, but they're not going to make it easy for you."

Nora called her program officer at National Geographic. "I called him from the field, and I was shaking. I had waited a year and a half for this permit, and now everything was just falling apart. I didn't know what to do. If I dug at the site, I'd be risking the safety of my team." Plus, Nora worried that if they did discover important artifacts, a local gang might chase them off, loot the site, and sell the goods. Then the information she needed to understand the history of the place would be lost forever.

"In everything we do, there's always some risk," Nora says, "but you can control the amount of risk you want to take. I decided that my first excavation as a director should not be doing something so dangerous." It was a difficult decision, but Nora called off the dig in Tell Zuwelen. She filed for a new permit, to dig at a site near a village she was more familiar with, and where she knew many of the people. This site was called Tell Timai, and it included the ruins of the Greco-Roman Egyptian city of Thmuis, which was a bustling and powerful city from about 400 B.C. to A.D. 800.

She waited another 12 months for the new permit to come through, but once her dig finally got underway, everything went just fine. "This really ended up being a much better place for me to lead my first dig," she says. "Sometimes, when things seem to be falling to pieces, everything is actually falling into place."

She worked closely with two villagers who knew archaeological work inside and out. "They come from a long history of archaeologists," she says, "and I learned so much from them." Together they created an illustrated, cartoon-style book to explain their work to the children of the village.

"You know, everyone thinks we're digging for gold," Nora says, "and that's not what we're doing at all. Those tiny, tiny pottery sherds we excavate actually help us date the site, because each Egyptian dynasty had its own particular pottery style." Nora gave copies of the book to the local schools and libraries. She gave them to the police officers who were working so hard every day to guard them and said, "These are for your children." All the kids in town seemed to love the book, but it was even more popular with the adults. "It was the biggest hit ever," Nora says. "They'd actually had no idea of the historical significance of the area where they were born. Now the villagers felt proud to understand that this was their history."

And there is so much more to find out! "Most people think that historians have already discovered everything there is to know about ancient Egypt," Nora says. "This is not true. Even with all the discoveries in the news every day, we've just barely begun to scratch the surface. It's more accurate to imagine our work like a giant jigsaw puzzle: As archaeologists, we're always excavating tiny puzzle pieces and then trying to put them all together, to understand the bigger picture." As Nora works to complete her Ph.D., in a joint program at Cairo University in Egypt and Durham University in England, she'll be supervising crews at this site again and again, discovering new pieces each year and slowly putting them together to reveal the ancient history of the ordinary people of Tell Timai.

> " Sometimes, when things seem to be falling to pieces, everything is actually falling into place. "

NORA AND HER TEAM ADJUST THEIR MAGNETOMETER, A TOOL THAT LETS THEM SEE UNDERGROUND STRUCTURES.

One of Nora's all-time favorite finds was an ancient necklace made of lapis lazuli, a rare and expensive blue stone. The necklace was still around an ancient skeleton's neck!

NORA AND A COLLEAGUE EXCAVATE A WALL AT TELL TIMAI, EGYPT.

# INSPIRATION STATION
## Nora's Advice for Aspiring Archaeologists

"Even if you get rejected, be persistent, become resilient, and stay focused. Rejection will mold you and push you and make you grow. If people say you can't do something—be the first to do it! Keep pushing forward, and set goals for yourself. Most important, if you have something to say, speak up, and speak loudly. Being a woman has give me some challenges, especially in regions where it isn't so common to see a woman in the field, but women are now communicating their science more often. That's helping to create more opportunities and more acceptance for women, and you can be a part of that change."

## NORA'S MUST-HAVE

A trowel. That's a small tool used for digging. It's especially useful for pulling back layers of soil, to uncover the mudbrick that was used to build ancient structures.

# DIG IN!
## ANCIENT HISTORY UNEARTHED

The Nile River, which flows through northeastern Africa, is the longest river in the world. All along its serpentine shores lie hot spots of buried history. There, archaeologists have uncovered clues about what life was like thousands of years ago.

Europe
Asia
**NILE DELTA**
Africa
Atlantic Ocean
Indian Ocean

**Mediterranean Sea**

Thonis-Heracleion

*Nile Delta*

Pi-Ramesses

Bubastis

Suez Canal

E G Y P T

Memphis

*Nile River*

Gulf of Suez

## Thonis-Heracleion

This ancient sunken city was discovered in the year 2000 off the coast of Egypt in the Mediterranean Sea, 30 feet (9 m) below the surface. Thought to have been an important trade hub and religious center, the site's fascinating finds include giant statues, gold coins, remains of shipwrecks, amulets, ceramics, and more.

**THIS LIMESTONE HOLDER CONTAINS ANCIENT GOLD FRAGMENTS.**

## Pi-Ramesses

During part of the 13th century B.C., this city was the capital of Egypt. Archaeologists have uncovered many artifacts, including cuneiform tablets, a large building complex equal to the size of about six football fields, and even children's footprints, immortalized in cement.

MUSEUMGOERS VISIT A MASSIVE STATUE OF PHARAOH RAMESSES II, WHO OVERSAW THE BUILDING OF PI-RAMESSES.

## Bubastis

In this important city, more than 2,000 years ago, pharaohs built a spectacular temple for Bastet, the cat goddess said to protect the home from evil spirits and disease. When archaeologists discovered the Temple Bastet, they found more than 600 cat statues inside it.

## Memphis

Founded around 2925 B.C. by King Menes, this city was mostly hidden underground when archaeologists began exploring it in the 19th century. In ancient times, Memphis was considered one of the greatest cities in the world. Today, the site is celebrated for the incredible discoveries that have been made there, including an ornate palace, huge sun temples, more than a dozen pyramids, and more than 9,000 rock-cut tombs, like the one discovered recently belonging to Queen Neit.

DJOSER'S STEP PYRAMID, LOCATED JUST OUTSIDE MEMPHIS, IS THOUGHT TO BE ANCIENT EGYPT'S OLDEST PYRAMID TOMB.

St. Louis, Missouri, U.S.A.

# DANIELLE N. LEE

# MAMMOLOGIST AND OUTREACH SCIENTIST

A mammologist is a biologist who studies mammals—their physical traits, behaviors, and ecology. Outreach scientists help others, especially young students, get interested in and understand their field of study, and they help illuminate pathways into science.

**W**hen biologist Dr. Danielle N. Lee was a little girl, in Memphis, Tennessee, U.S.A., she was curious about *everything*, but especially about animals. She had no shortage of questions about cats, dogs, and the wild animals she'd seen on nature shows like *Wild Kingdom*. "The questions I asked as a child were kind of the same questions I'm asking now," Danielle says. "*What are they doing? Why do they do that? How do they do that?* I was always very curious."

Danielle knew from a young age that she wanted to work with animals in her career. She decided to set her sights on becoming a veterinarian. "I didn't comprehend that there were biologists or wildlife ecologists," she says. "I literally thought all professionals who worked with animals were veterinarians. I had no idea the diversity of careers that were possible."

Veterinary school, though, is highly competitive, and when Danielle didn't get accepted, she decided to begin classes as part of a master's degree program in biology. She hoped that would make her a stronger candidate when she applied the next time. After one of her professors read a paper she'd written as part of a weekly assignment, he encouraged her to turn it into a full-fledged research project. Her professor saw something special in her work. He said to her, "You ask good questions. You can really do this!" While Danielle thought a research project sounded like fun, she never imagined that the questions she'd been asking her whole life could lead to a career.

Instead of going to veterinary school, Danielle's professor encouraged her to get a biology degree and become a college professor. Danielle could hardly believe her ears: "What!? You mean I'd get to study animal behavior all day? I'd get paid to watch animals!?" she asked him. His answer? Yes!

"To my professors in college, my teachers in high school—I was always asking, *Why, why, why?*" Danielle says. "Up until then, I thought the answers came from somewhere or someone else. But it was then that I realized I could answer my own questions." It was a lightbulb moment for Danielle. She didn't have to be a veterinarian to work with animals. She could be a scientist, or more specifically, a mammologist. She says she realized then and there, "This is what I want to do."

Becoming a scientist wasn't something Danielle had ever considered before, perhaps because she hadn't seen scientists who looked like her when she was a kid. When she'd thought of a scientist as she was growing up, she'd pictured a white man. While there are more women and people of color in the field today, Danielle still deals with many people who have a specific idea of what a scientist looks like.

"Even when someone knows that a scientist will be coming by, I'll show up and they'll say, 'We're waiting on a scientist,'" she says. "I say, 'That's me.

I'm the scientist.' Even today, we still have to educate people that scientists come in different packages."

Danielle wants to make sure young people know that there isn't only one kind of person who can do what she does. As long as you are curious, ask questions, and want to investigate the answers, you can become a scientist. So, when Danielle was in graduate school, she helped organize an after-school biology club for high school students in St. Louis, Missouri. When it came to observing wildlife, most of the students felt that everything exciting and interesting happened in places far away—places none of them would ever get to.

"At that time, even I hadn't fully registered the variety of wildlife that was literally right outside our door, and the science that could be done there," Danielle says. "I'd spent most of my youth outside, and I could tell you the names of all the plants and animals in my neighborhood, but for some reason I didn't think that could form the basis of a valuable scientific study. Doing outreach with these kids— that's what got me to start looking more closely at the nature right in my own backyard."

Danielle and her students began catching birds and "banding" them, which is what it's called when scientists put a band around a bird's leg—each with a unique set of numbers—to keep track of them and observe their movements over time. They also identified all the trees on campus and visited local nature areas, cataloging which species lived there. From this beginning, Danielle helped develop a summer research program focusing on urban ecology.

The outreach program inspired her to study urban ecology in her own research, too. After getting the program up and running and earning her Ph.D., Danielle began to focus her own work on mice, rats, and other backyard rodents.

"We want to understand how the same species can successfully live across so many different situations," Danielle says. "Rodents are notorious for making a living out of anything. As a group, they're tenacious and have done an amazing job of surviving." Danielle and her colleagues study rodents that live in cities and rodents that live in rural

> " It was then that I realized I could answer my own questions. "

environments. "We're trying to understand what makes them the same and what makes them different." It's important work: Understanding rats and their lifestyles can help maintain the health of the people and communities who interact with them.

Today, Danielle works both near home—in and around the city of St. Louis—where she studies field mice, and abroad in Tanzania, where she studies giant pouched rats. In Tanzania, just as in the United States, Danielle feels her difference or "otherness," but there it's "a different kind of 'other,'" she says. "There, I'm a woman doing [what is considered to be] a man's work. And once I speak with them, they realize I'm not African either. Then they're even more surprised! For many people, particularly in the rural parts, I'm the first Afro-American they've ever met."

But despite these challenges, Danielle is determined. She is passionate about pushing past boundaries and inspiring young people of all backgrounds to get engaged in science. Because for Danielle, science is a bridge that unites people, regardless of their differences, in investigating and discovering the amazing world around them.

## INSPIRATION STATION
### Danielle's Advice for Aspiring Biologists

"For many science careers, you have to go to college. And the most important thing is to make sure you finish college. So the most practical advice I can give a young person is, make sure to apply for enough scholarships before graduating from high school. A main reason we don't have underrepresented minorities in a lot of these careers is because they run out of finances and can't finish school. I could say a lot of inspirational stuff, but inspiration means nothing if you don't have the support in place to finish college."

♡ ⚬⚬⚬ 🔍

# RATS TO THE RESCUE!

African giant pouched rats are about the size of a house cat and have pouches in their cheeks, which they love to stuff with corn or nuts or whatever crop is in season. They're fast, skilled climbers, and these big rodents can sometimes be a big annoyance, like when they invade peoples' homes or eat the food grown by farmers. But they also have the potential to do a lot of good: They have a keen sense of smell, and they're very intelligent. In fact, Danielle first began working with pouched rats at an organization funded by the U.S. Department of Defense, which trains them to sniff out land mines, much like bomb-sniffing dogs!

Rats can squeeze through tiny openings just over a half-inch (1.3 cm) wide.

A rat's brain is smaller and simpler than a human's, but it functions very similarly.

A yellow-rumped leaf-eared mouse was found living more than 22,000 feet (6,700 m) above sea level, at the top of a volcano in South America, making it the world's highest-dwelling mammal.

# ASKING GOOD QUESTIONS—
# AND SEEKING ANSWERS

## DESIGNING AN EXPERIMENT USING THE SCIENTIFIC METHOD

To learn more about the natural world, scientists like Danielle use the scientific method, which is a way of designing experiments to answer questions.

### CHECK OUT HOW IT WORKS IN A REAL EXAMPLE: ONE OF DANIELLE'S STUDIES.

**1** **Identify a Good Question:** A good scientific question is one that can be tested, meaning you can measure the results by collecting evidence. Danielle wanted to know: How are mice that live in urban areas different from and the same as mice that live in rural areas?

**2** **Conduct Research:** During this step, you study and try to find out as much as you can about the topics that you'll be investigating.

**3** **Make a Hypothesis:** A hypothesis is an educated guess about what you think the results of your experiment will be. Danielle's hypothesis was that the types of mice—as well as how they look and behave—would vary in different environments.

**4** **Conduct an Experiment:** Here's the plan Danielle and her colleagues made to test their hypothesis.

- *Catch some mice.* Each day at dusk, Danielle and her teammates set traps (designed not to hurt the mice) in different locations. Then, they would go back in the morning to see what sort of critters they'd caught.

- *Identify the species.* When they caught a mouse (or two or three), each one was given a unique identification number, either on a microchip or a small tag that was put on its ear. Then, they determined what kind of mouse it was. Some of the types Danielle expected to find were house mice, deer mice, and jumping mice.

- *Record their traits.* Danielle and her colleagues documented specific information about each mouse, including its weight, length, and behavior, and whether or not it had a common mouse-borne infection called *Salmonella*.

**5** **Draw a Conclusion:** After conducting your experiment, use the evidence you've collected to answer the original question. It can take years to complete a scientific study, and Danielle is still working to answer her original question.

# JEAN
# BEASLEY

Topsail Island,
North Carolina,
U.S.A.

In 1970, on a moonlit night on Topsail Island, North Carolina, U.S.A., Jean Beasley's brother called her to the beach. There was something huge coming out of the water, and he knew Jean needed to see it, too.

Jean and her family ran to the beach and watched in awe as a loggerhead sea turtle slid out of the water, not far from their feet. They observed as the mother turtle made her way up the beach, found just the right spot, dug a hole, laid her eggs, carefully covered the hole, then braved the breaking waves to make her way back out to sea. "It was breathtaking," says Jean. "It was a moment of magic."

That moment was the spark that ignited Jean's decades-long passion for sea turtle rescue. Her journey began very practically, with a visit to the local library to read more about sea turtles. Then, in the years following, she and other interested neighbors began marking off sea turtle nests to make sure beachgoers didn't accidentally harm them. For thousands of years, female loggerhead sea turtles have returned each summer to the sandy beaches around Topsail Island to dig nests and lay eggs. But in the last few decades, as developers have built more houses and hotels in places that were once turtle habitat, the reptiles have had much less space to build their nests.

Over the years, the group of volunteers grew. Eventually, Jean retired from her career as a teacher and school administrator. Now she had more time to walk the beaches of Topsail, looking for tracks, or turtles that had been injured by boats or tangled in fishing nets. It was on one of her beach walks that Jean first spotted a badly injured loggerhead—a turtle that would change her life forever.

The turtle had a big gash on its forehead as well as other cuts and bruises. *It must have been hit by a boat,* Jean thought. She knew she had to get this animal medical attention, and fast. But there was nowhere nearby to take an injured turtle. So she and some fellow volunteers drove the turtle to the veterinary school at North Carolina State University, more than two hours away. Jean knew a vet there who could help. After he addressed the worst of the turtle's injuries, Jean breathed a sigh of relief. She knew, though, that the poor turtle would be recovering from its wounds for a long time, so she asked the doctor if she could come back and visit it later.

"Visit!?" he laughed. "No—the turtle's going back with you. We have no place to take care of a sea turtle." Well, neither did Jean Beasley! But she didn't let that deter her. She put the turtle, which they named Lucky, in a big washtub in her basement for a day, while another volunteer located a used tank from a state aquarium. She and some of the volunteers patched it up, placed it in a neighbor's backyard, and filled it with water. Now the turtle had a small, safe space in which to recover.

Lucky taught Jean and the other volunteers a lot about sea turtles. "That turtle was so patient with us," says Jean. "We used to feed Lucky five times a day because we thought it needed to eat a lot to get well. He would look at us like, 'Oh no, not again. Here they come with the food!'" Nevertheless, Lucky was one well-loved (and well-fed) loggerhead. He recovered and was released back into the ocean.

As it turns out, Lucky was the first of many sea turtles to be helped by Jean and the other dedicated volunteers. The very next summer, they rescued four more turtles. As more and more of the animals arrived, the group needed more space to house and take care of them all. Jean asked the town of Topsail Beach if she could rent an empty plot of land. Much to Jean's delight, the town said yes, and that she would be charged only one dollar a year for rent. Twenty-seven years after she saw her first sea turtle, Jean established the Karen Beasley Sea Turtle Rescue and Rehabilitation Center. It was named after her daughter, who, before she passed away from leukemia, had also been a leader in local sea turtle rehabilitation

## CITIZEN SCIENTIST

Citizen scientists are everyday people who do scientific research, or other kinds of volunteer work, usually for or with a scientist or scientific organization.

efforts. It was the first sea turtle hospital north of the Florida Keys!

Over the years since then, the hospital has grown. In 2013, the center outgrew its first building and moved in to a larger one, in the nearby town of Surf City. The new facility has a fully equipped operating room, an intensive care unit, and a huge recovery room, where the turtles can get better before being released. So far, Jean and her crew of volunteers have treated and released more than 1,500 turtles. "You learn what you love," she says. "If you're interested in something, you'll find a way to learn about it. And the learning will lead to doing."

Today, wildlife rehabilitators and interested visitors come from around the world to see the center and learn about sea turtles from Jean and her volunteers. Jean spends a lot of time teaching and talking to people about how human behavior impacts the environment and can harm sea turtles.

"These are ancient animals that evolved before the time of the dinosaurs," she says. "They have survived all the cataclysmic events that have shaped and reshaped our planet, but they are not surviving what we humans are doing to them."

Turtles come to the center with many different kinds of injuries, most of which are caused by human activities. They are hit by boats and tangled in nets, and some have accidentally swallowed barbed fishing hooks. Another monumental problem for turtles—as well as other sea creatures—is plastic pollution. A plastic bag floating in the water looks very similar to a jellyfish. It's not uncommon for turtles to arrive at the center with their stomachs blocked by plastic they've accidentally eaten. For Jean and the other volunteers, the work can sometimes feel overwhelming. "If we ever start to falter, though," says Jean, "I feel Lucky's flipper on my back saying, 'You keep going!'"

About 90 percent of the turtles that are brought to the center get better, and when they do, they're released back into the ocean. "When we return them to the sea," says Jean, "it is an emotional moment." As the volunteers carry the

healthy turtles back toward the ocean, the turtles start to get very excited. They hear the familiar swoosh of the waves and smell the salt air. They lift their heads and flap their flippers. "When you take them to the water, and let them go, many times they turn around and look at you, as if they're saying goodbye," says Jean. "We know we're sending them back to the place they came from. Back to the place they belong. But back into the same dangers that brought them to the hospital; so, it is an emotional moment."

Many visitors come to watch when the turtles are released. "The turtles we care for all have names, we nurse them, and we love them," Jean says. "Every one we release takes a little piece of our heart away with them. But there is something so rewarding and so inspiring about bringing that turtle from near death back to life."

Jean sees the work she does helping sea turtles as one part of a very large effort to help the environment. "The sea turtles are trying to tell us something," Jean says, "and we need to pay attention. If they are doing badly, then we are all doing badly. Every living thing needs a clean and safe environment. The turtles' message is that we must do something to change how we are treating this planet."

> "There is something so rewarding and so inspiring about bringing that turtle from near death back to life.

Sea turtles can detect the invisible lines of Earth's magnetic field. A female turtle can find her way back to the beach where she was born by remembering its unique magnetic signature.

♡ ⚬⚬⚬ 🔍

## THE TURTLE CIRCLE OF LIFE

The start of a sea turtle's life is a bit like an epic adventure—filled with long, tiring journeys, dangerous predators, and exhausting obstacles (like big, breaking waves). Scientists estimate that only 1 in 5,000 to 10,000 will live the 20 to 30 years it takes to become a mature adult. Sea turtles spend most of their life in the ocean. The females only come ashore to lay their eggs—usually returning to the same beach, or even the same area of the beach, where they were born. In North Carolina, loggerhead turtles nest from mid-May through August. Each female may come ashore three to five times during one season, laying about 120 eggs per nest. The eggs take about 60 days to hatch. When they do, hundreds of tiny turtles race to the sea. Hungry birds, ghost crabs, and other predators snap up many before they make it to the water, where still more dangers lurk. But the remarkable reptiles push on, determined to reach what will be their new home—the deep blue sea.

♥ ⚬⚬⚬ 🔍

## INSPIRATION STATION
### Jean's Advice for Aspiring Wildlife Rehabilitators

"One: Always be ready to step into the unknown. If you're presented with an opportunity you can learn from, you should never be afraid to give it a try. Two: Spend more time outdoors and learn about the Earth. Even if it is just around your home or school—take every opportunity to look. Look at what is growing there and what is living there. Every tree, every bird, every bug, every type of grass is important."

Turtle excluder devices (or TEDs) are trapdoor-like openings at the bottom of fishing nets to help trapped turtles escape.

# YOU CAN HELP

## BE PART OF THE PLASTIC POLLUTION SOLUTION

One of the greatest threats facing our oceans, as well as the wildlife living within them, is plastic pollution. It's estimated that up to 12 million tons (10.8 million t) of plastic wind up in the oceans each year. Most of this plastic waste comes from trash thrown on the ground or into rivers, which then gets blown or washed into the sea. Millions of animals—including sea turtles—are killed by plastic each year. They get tangled in it, or they eat it, thinking it's a jellyfish, seagrass, or some other tasty-looking sea treat. So there's no doubt about it: We have a plastic problem. But the good news is, no matter who you are and no matter where you live, you can be a part of the solution. Here are four ways to get started.

## 1 Do a plastic pickup with family, friends, and neighbors.

Whether you live by an ocean, lake, river, or city park, gather some people (including a parent or guardian), pick a spot in nature, and pick up all the trash and plastic you can find. Don't forget to bring gloves!

A recent study found that over half of all sea turtles have eaten plastic in their lifetime.

## 2 Say no to single-use plastic.

Single-use plastic is plastic you use once and then throw away, like plastic water bottles, forks, and bags. And there are lots of ways to use less of it. For example, bring reusable shopping bags to the store, skip plastic straws, invest in a reusable water bottle, and consider writing your favorite restaurant to suggest swapping out plastic utensils for bamboo or metal alternatives.

## 3 Make sure your family and school are recycling.

Does everyone in your family and school know which items are recyclable and where they should go? If not, make sure everyone has the info they need to be an environmental protector.

## 4 Donate your old plastic toys.

Instead of throwing away your old plastic toys—sending them to already stuffed landfills—donate them so they can be used again!

PLASTIC Please Recycle

GLASS Please Recycle

CANS Please Recycle

PAPER Please Recycle

# CAROLINA
## FREITAS

It was the middle of the night, deep in the Amazon rainforest. Dr. Carolina Freitas was traveling down a shallow stream in a small wooden canoe with a group of fishers. All she could see was what was lit by the small bulb in her headlamp. But she knew what was out there. And what was out there was making her a bit nervous.

"I thought, *If we turn this canoe, how will I get out of here?*" Carolina says. For starters, she knew that both banks of the stream were lined with caimans, a reptile related to alligators and crocodiles. "I was looking at both banks and thinking, *Which one is closer to me?* But there were so many caimans, I thought I might not arrive there alive if the canoe capsized."

Carolina was on this midnight expedition in search of the arapaima—the largest scaled freshwater fish in the world. She is an ecologist who studies the relationship between human activities and the other living things in the environment. Currently, she is studying how people who live along the river in Amazonia have helped the arapaima population go from endangered to growing again.

Native to the rivers and lakes of the Amazon Basin in South America, arapaimas can grow to be more than nine feet (2.75 m) long and weigh up to 440 pounds (200 kg). In addition to its sharp, bony teeth, an arapaima has teeth on the roof of its mouth, which it uses to shred its prey. These fish are incredibly important to Amazonian communities. The people who sell them depend on them for income. Many people love to eat them. Their scales are sometimes used for jewelry, and their bony tongues can be used as a scraping tool.

First, humans were impacting these fish in a negative way. Overfishing and habitat loss caused arapaimas to disappear from many parts of the basin, and in other parts their numbers are still decreasing rapidly. But then, in the 1990s, afraid that these important fish were going to go extinct, the Amazonas state government in Brazil made fishing for them illegal. Still, some people continued to catch them, even though the law said not to. Arapaima populations continued to decline.

At the beginning of the 2000s, a nonprofit organization worked together with the local people to create a long-term plan to help conserve the fish and allowed licensed communities to legally begin catching arapaimas again. The plan includes rules to make sure the arapaima population continues to grow. For example, there are certain places where arapaima fishing is allowed and others where it's off-limits and the fish can grow and breed unbothered. And depending on the number of arapaima in each lake, a limit is set as to how many arapaimas can be caught each year.

Even though Carolina grew up in Brazil, before she began her career as a

> **"**
> In school, I'd gotten used to thinking of people as a problem for nature.
> **"**

researcher, she'd never been to the Amazon. "One thing I learned when I went to the Amazon is that water landscapes are everywhere," Carolina says. "You move by water, and all the rivers are different. In other parts of Brazil, we use roads to move from one city to another. But there, it's rivers."

To get to the communities she works with, Carolina flies to a nearby city and then travels by boat. It often takes her a few hours to travel from one community to the next. During her fieldwork, which usually takes one to three months, she lives on a boat most of the time, sleeping in a hammock, and listening to the sounds of the rainforest at night. "You can see a lot of caimans, freshwater river dolphins, and many birds," Carolina says. "And sometimes you can see macaws and even monkeys."

Talking with the people in these isolated communities and observing their daily lives changed Carolina's whole view of life. "In school, I'd gotten used to thinking of people as a problem for nature," she says. Now she sees them as part of the solution. In communities that practice arapaima management, local fishers manage the entire process. One important aspect of their job is to keep track of the number of arapaimas in their lakes and waterways. But arapaimas normally live in muddy or black waters, where it's almost impossible to see them. So how exactly do they get an accurate count? As it turns out, the local fishers have a special skill.

Arapaimas have an unusual trait among fish: Much like whales and dolphins, they come to the surface to breathe atmospheric air. Today, the local fishers often use nets to catch the fish, but many grew up using the traditional method of harpooning arapaimas from their canoes. To do that, they would watch and listen for a fish to surface and then, based on what they've learned about the fish's behavior, predict where it would surface next. These days they're using this same tactic to count the arapaimas and keep track of them. With information carefully gathered from interviews with local fishers, Carolina is trying to understand how different populations of arapaima have changed over time, and how well the plan to conserve them has been working on a larger scale.

To conduct her research, Carolina accompanies the fishers during the arapaima harvest, which, in some communities, occurs in the middle of the night. She's often struck by how completely at ease the fishers and their families are in the environment. "I saw kids working together with their parents—little kids, four and five years old," she says. "Even if it's two in the morning, they all want to be there, to learn and participate—to pull in those nets and see what they've caught."

Today, Carolina can actually hear the difference between a lake in a community that's managing their fish, and lakes in communities that are not. "When the arapaima comes to the surface to breathe, they make a sound," Carolina says. "When you go to a lake where they have a community-based management plan, you hear the fish, like *pow!* It sounds like fireworks are going off. You feel that the whole lake is alive! But when you go to a place where they don't have management, you don't hear anything. It's completely quiet."

The communities that are enacting arapaima management are well organized and passionately involved in the management of their own resources. Everyone in the community takes part in the planning, and in most places, their plans are working very well. Season by season, day by day, these people are figuring out ways of living sustainably in their environment. What Carolina wants most now is to help spread this success to as many Amazonian communities as possible, so they too can hear the arapaima fireworks again.

## INSPIRATION STATION
### Carolina's Advice for Aspiring Ecologists

"You need to keep going, no matter what people say. Many times, academic conservationists are not open to new ideas, and they may try to make you give up. But more and more, they are realizing how important it is to include local people in conservation. In school, when professors and colleagues have criticized my work, I've had moments when I was sad and even considered quitting. But as soon as I am in the field, all that doubt vanishes. I'm always happy—even when the mosquitoes make it difficult!"

FISHERS HOLD UP AN ARAPAIMA.

Arapaimas eat other fish, seeds, fruits, and insects. The fish opens its large mouth, creating a vacuum that sucks its meal in.

CAROLINA INTERVIEWS A FISHER.

👀 CAROLINA'S
## MUST-HAVE
A hammock. And a mosquito net that attaches to the hammock, so that she's not bitten while she sleeps.

CAROLINA POSES WITH ARAPAIMAS CAUGHT WITHIN A MANAGED AREA.

The waters where arapaimas live are very low in oxygen. They've adapted to this problem by evolving the ability to breathe atmospheric air.

# ANIMALS OF AMAZONIA

The Amazon River stretches at least 4,000 miles (6,437 km), from high in the Andes mountain range in Peru down to the north coast of Brazil, where it flows into the Atlantic Ocean. The arapaima is just one of many unique animals that live in this amazing ecosystem. It's home to incredible plant and animal diversity, and many of the species slithering, crawling, swimming, and flying nearby have yet to be discovered.

**Here are a few of the wild, wonderful creatures that call the Amazon River home.**

## Black Caiman

A relative of alligators, black caimans grow up to 16 feet (4.9 m) long and weigh more than 800 pounds (363 kg)! They eat fish, other reptiles, and rodents—like capybaras—with their more than 70 teeth.

## Green Anaconda

Weighing in at a whopping 550 pounds (250 kg) and sometimes stretching 30 feet (9 m) long, these are the largest snakes in the world. They have super-stretchy jaws that allow them to swallow their prey whole, and after a big meal—of, say, a wild pig, a deer, or even a jaguar—they can go weeks or months without eating again.

## Electric Eel

These fish get their name from—you guessed it—their ability to emit a large electric charge. With it, they can stun their prey (and scare off their predators). Electric eels can grow to be six to eight feet (1.8–2.5 m) long and weigh up to 44 pounds (20 kg).

## Capybara

The world's biggest rodent, capybaras can eat up to eight pounds (3.6 kg) of grass each day. And if that's not weird enough, they also eat their own poop in the mornings, because it's so rich in protein!

## Matamata Turtle

The matamata is one strange-looking turtle! It has a rough, knobby shell; a flat, triangular head; and a wide neck that is covered with warts and ridges. Its long, tubelike snout works like a snorkel, poking out of the water so that the turtle can breathe while it swims below the surface.

## Red-Bellied Piranha

These little fish pack a mighty punch. They have strong jaws and triangular, razor-sharp teeth that they use to eat little chunks out of other fish's bodies and tails. They often hunt in groups of up to 100 fish, each one taking a bite out of the same prey.

# MUNAZZA ALAM

MUNAZZA ALAM (CENTER) STANDS WITH HER COLLEAGUES HALEY FICA (LEFT) AND SARA CAMNASIO (RIGHT) IN FRONT OF A 21-FOOT (6.4-M)-WIDE TELESCOPE IN CHILE.

## ASTRONOMER

Astronomers study the universe and everything in it, including the stars, moons and planets in our solar system, and the planets in orbit around other stars.

Humans have long looked up at the sky and wondered: Are we alone in the universe? Astronomers have discovered thousands of planets, orbiting distant stars, but are any of them like our Earth? Could any support life? That's what astronomer Munazza Alam wants to find out.

To do that, Munazza travels to observatories around the world, using giant telescopes to peek into weather on other worlds. One crucial factor for life on Earth is our life-sustaining atmosphere—made up of nitrogen, oxygen, water vapor, dust, and other gases. If she can identify what makes up other planets' atmospheres, Munazza may be able to tell how likely it is that those planets could sustain life, too.

Munazza's first research trip was in college—to the Kitt Peak National Observatory, high on a mountaintop in Arizona's Sonoran Desert. "I was a kid from New York City, and I'd never seen the night sky like that," Munazza says. In large cities, light pollution often muddies the night sky, making it difficult to see stars. "Where I could see maybe two stars at home, here I could see hundreds of thousands. It was so impressive!"

Munazza was hooked. She knew then and there that astronomy would become her life's work. She decided to major in physics, with a focus in astronomy. Out of the 30 students in her college's physics program, only three were women. Still, in a field where it's easy for a woman to feel alone and outnumbered, Munazza feels lucky to have had supportive women in her life, in many different roles.

One such woman was her college adviser, who took Munazza's interests seriously and helped her connect with yet another inspiring woman, a professor who was running an astronomy research group at the Smithsonian American Museum of Natural History. Munazza joined her research team and remained a member all through college. She got to know many of her fellow astronomy students there, and it was there that she met her friend, Sara.

"It was so great to have my duo with Sara," Munazza says. "We were in all the same classes, so

> **"** One of the things that has kept me going through hard times is to have an arsenal of strong women role models and peers who inspire me. **"**

we battled our homework assignments together, we worked on research projects together, and we traveled together, too. Our friendship has been a great support system for both of us."

When her father faced life-saving surgery, Munazza's relationship with Sara kept her going. "It was one of the most difficult things I'd ever faced," Munazza says. Having a kind and compassionate friend, as well as an understanding adviser, made all the difference. Thanks to their support, Munazza persisted and went on to graduate school.

Today, she leads research projects of her own, as she observes and measures the atmospheres of planets outside our solar system. "We call these exoplanets," Munazza says. To discover them, Munazza makes use of data collected by the Hubble Space Telescope, which was sent into orbit around Earth in 1990. The Hubble telescope collects light from stars and planets and sends the information back to scientists on Earth. Once new exoplanets are discovered, Munazza travels to observatories that house high-resolution telescopes in remote (and dark!) locations, such as Arizona's Kitt Peak, or Las Campanas in Chile's Atacama Desert. She also studies the stars that these planets orbit to better understand how they formed.

The trip to Las Campanas from Munazza's office in Cambridge, Massachusetts, takes 24 hours and includes four plane rides. From the airport in the little Chilean town of La Serena, it's a two-hour drive across the vast brownish red sands of the desert and then up along a mountain ridge, so high you leave the clouds below. For Munazza, standing on that mountain, more than 7,800 feet (2,377 m) above sea level, and looking up at the clear, bright, star-speckled sky is always a huge thrill and an inspiration. But although astronomers come from all around the world to use the big telescopes there, most of the time when Munazza is on site she is the only woman.

Munazza hopes that will soon be different. "One of the things that has kept me going through hard times is to have an arsenal of strong women role models and peers who inspire me and keep me going," she says. While the number of women pursuing careers in physics and astronomy is increasing over time, they are still underrepresented in these fields. Munazza hopes that in the future many more women will join her and her female colleagues on that mountaintop. While she continues to search for evidence that we are not alone in the universe, she will continue to stand up as a mentor to young girls and women who aspire to become astronomers themselves, so they never have to feel alone in their field.

## INSPIRATION STATION
### Munazza's Advice for Aspiring Astronomers

"If you have any questions, ask, and ask again. It's not a bad thing to be curious. Wondering how things work and thinking about how something could be better or different is a great way to see the world, and it can help us see beyond the surface. A lot of important discoveries in history came about because someone was curious— because someone asked a question. You should ask questions, too! You never know what important discovery the answer might lead to!"

The world's giant telescopes are usually located at high elevations or in areas that get little rainfall. Being up where the air is thin and where there are few clouds makes for the best visibility.

## MUNAZZA'S MUST-HAVE

Lip balm and hand cream. The deserts and high mountaintops where big telescopes are located are always very dry.

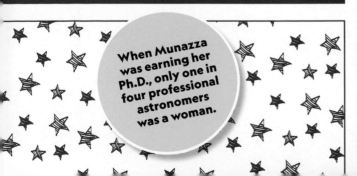

When Munazza was earning her Ph.D., only one in four professional astronomers was a woman.

# LOOK UP!

## Simple Ways to Explore the Night Sky

Staring up at the night sky, wondering what's out there, and being totally amazed by our relative smallness in the universe is time well spent. Grab a blanket, binoculars if you have them, and an adult. Spend a little time outside, just looking up. Even without a giant telescope, you're sure to be enchanted. Here are some more tips for making the most of time spent under the stars.

### 1

**Watch the weather.**
Choose a night that is totally clear, with no clouds in the sky.

### 2

**Seek out the dark.**
That's where visibility will be the best. Finding a dark place will be harder for people living in cities, so just do the best you can. Try going to a park or near a river or lake to see if you can see more of the sky there.

### 3

**Notice how the sky changes.**
Because Earth rotates on its axis, we see stars in different positions each night, appearing to move across the sky. And because Earth revolves around the sun, we see different parts of the sky at different times of year.

## Look for planets.

To spot planets from Earth, first find the ecliptic, which is the path that the sun, moon, and planets take across the sky. During the day, take notice of the path that the sun takes, then look there at night for planets. Unlike stars, planets don't twinkle.

**4**

## Look for a constellation.

A constellation is a group of stars that make up an imaginary outline of a shape or figure. Most of the constellations that we know today were named in ancient times by people in Greece, Rome, and the Middle East. Before you go out, do some research on constellations, pick one that you like the most, then try to find it in the night sky.

**5**

## Gaze at the moon.

Notice how the moon's shape changes each night, growing from a tiny sliver to a full moon and then back again over the course of about a month. The moon orbits Earth, and Earth orbits the sun, so how much we see of the moon depends on its position between Earth and the sun. The dark spots that we can see on the moon—called maria— are large craters filled with now hardened lava.

**6**

**7**

## Look for shooting stars.

A shooting star is actually a meteor (or space rock) hurtling through space that burns up as it enters Earth's atmosphere. In dark conditions, on average, you can see a shooting star every 10 to 15 minutes. During meteor showers, you'll see many, many more!

Socotra,
Yemen

# ELLA
# AL-SHAMAHI

Once upon a time, Ella Al-Shamahi says, "there was more than one species of human walking the Earth. And now, we're the only ones left. Why is that?" In fact, there were several species of early humans, and yet the only species remaining is ours—*Homo sapiens*. As a paleoanthropologist, Ella studies clues from the distant past to find out more about those different species, and one in particular—Neanderthal, or *Homo neanderthalensis*, our closest extinct human relative.

To find out about those early human species, paleoanthropologists explore remote landscapes, searching for fossils. For Ella, the most fascinating places to explore are caves. "Caves were the original prime real estate," she says. "Caves are where humans originally used to live, so they can be a real treasure trove of information." What makes what Ella does so exciting, she says, is that "somebody might walk into a cave tomorrow and find a new species of human." And, as Ella points out, every little fossil clue could add a new piece to the mysterious, ever growing jigsaw puzzle that is, discovery by discovery, revealing the picture of our human family tree.

Some of the caves that have been explored the least are the ones with the most potential for exciting discoveries. And one reason some places haven't been explored very much yet—or at all—is that they're in locations where there is conflict or war, which makes them potentially dangerous to travel to and work in. These are the places that Ella is particularly interested in. "I work in unstable places because they are places where not as many people have looked," Ella says. "It would be a tragedy for science if people weren't looking there. It's also a tragedy for those places if science isn't being done there. It's important that the people and kids living there know that they can become scientists and that, potentially, the front line of science is on their doorstep."

Growing up, Ella became very curious about where humans came from. "I was just obsessed with human

## PALEOANTHROPOLOGIST

Paleoanthropologist = paleontologist + anthropologist. Paleoanthropologists study prehistoric humans. They look for and analyze fossil clues to find out about extinct human species and to discover the evolutionary origins of our own species.

evolution," she says. "Evolution can be quite controversial, and I think that was a huge part of what attracted me to it. The more I studied it, the more I dove deeper and deeper." In college, she started out studying genetics and then eventually made a sideways leap to paleoanthropology. The questions that most motivated her then are the same ones she studies today: Why are we the only species of humans left on Earth? How and when did *Homo sapiens* leave Africa, where they evolved? How many other species of humans existed?

*Homo sapiens* all originated in Africa, and there are two ways that they're thought to have traveled from the continent to other parts of the world: 1) By crossing through the Sinai Peninsula, which is part of Egypt and connects Africa to Asia; or 2) by crossing the Bab al Mandab strait, a narrow stretch of water between Africa and Yemen, a country in Asia.

Both of Ella's parents were born in Yemen. Although she grew up and went to college in Great Britain, she still has family who live in Yemen, and that helped Ella find ways to connect with local scientists. She was eager to travel to Yemen and check out the caves there. She wondered what clues she could unearth and what other species of early humans she might find. *What if there were a species hidden there not yet known to science?* But years of war and political strife have made the country dangerous, and many research teams have left the area.

Ella, though, wasn't going to give up. She was determined to find a way to explore Yemen. So she set her sights on a tiny group of islands off the coast of Yemen, called Socotra, which she had been told were safe once you arrived. In fact, there were even local and international scientists already working there.

"People call Socotra the most alien place on Earth," Ella says. It's also known as the Galápagos of the Indian Ocean because so many species of plants and animals live there that are found nowhere else in the world. There are a lot of sinkholes and caves on Socotra, and Ella wanted to help shine a light not only on the caves but also on the island's unique landforms and wildlife that are now endangered by warfare and ongoing political issues.

Finally, Ella got the OK to travel to Socotra. She and her team spent three days at sea, on a cement cargo ship that was crawling with cockroaches, carefully avoiding the pirates who frequent the dangerous waters. But when Ella finally laid eyes on the remote and magical islands, it was all worth it. "The trip felt like it had purpose," she says. "Emotionally, it was very important for me, because it was the first time I managed to get to the place where so much of my family is from."

The goal for the first trip was to identify potential caves that might be worth investigating further. "The first step when we arrived," she says, "was to walk the landscape and get tips from local people about which caves might be interesting." She and her team spent long hours searching the ground for stone tools, which could provide clues about the lives of Socotra's earliest inhabitants. They investigated several caves and identified some they hope may hold evidence of exactly when and how the first humans arrived on the island. The next step? Plan another trip back and start digging!

"There is no feeling on Earth like the start of an expedition," Ella once said. "It's that feeling when you jump out of a jeep, or you look up from a boat, and you know that there's this possibility—it's small, but it's still there—that you're about to find something that could add to or change our knowledge of who we are and where we come from. And it's a feeling that so many scientists have, but rarely in politically unstable places." Ella, though, is determined to change that. Starting with Yemen.

> "
>
> There is no feeling on Earth like the start of an expedition.
>
> "

Ella is also a stand-up comic. "Humor helps me cope with the darker aspects of my work in war-torn countries," she says. "But comedy also helps me communicate science. I do science stand-up at festivals around the world."

## ELLA'S MUST-HAVE

Her tool kit. It includes equipment like a trowel for digging, markers or pin flags for marking artifact bags, and antiseptic gel, to keep things clean.

# INSPIRATION STATION
## Ella's Advice for Aspiring Paleoanthropologists

"When I was growing up, I was told there were certain things that girls did and didn't do. Girls aren't adventurers, people said, girls shouldn't go out after dark, girls aren't engineers, girls are scaredy-cats. And I think—if I can do what I do, even though I was told all this stuff, then anyone who wants it can, too. If you enjoy something and you can turn it into your job, do it!"

# HOW HUMANS AND NEANDERTHALS STACK UP

Despite Neanderthals' small stature, a Neanderthal's brain was often the same size or larger than a modern human's brain.

Modern human skulls are rounder and more spherical, while Neanderthal skulls were longer and squatter, with a very distinctive, prominent ridge above the eyes.

Neanderthals had wider noses than *Homo sapiens*, which are thought to have helped them humidify and heat up the cold, dry air where they lived.

*Homo sapiens* have a much more pronounced chin than Neanderthals did.

# *Homo sapiens* vs. *Homo neanderthalensis*

Who were these early species of human, our closest extinct relative? Using DNA evidence and Neanderthal fossils, scientists are able to get a better picture of what made them similar and what set them apart from modern humans, *Homo sapiens*.

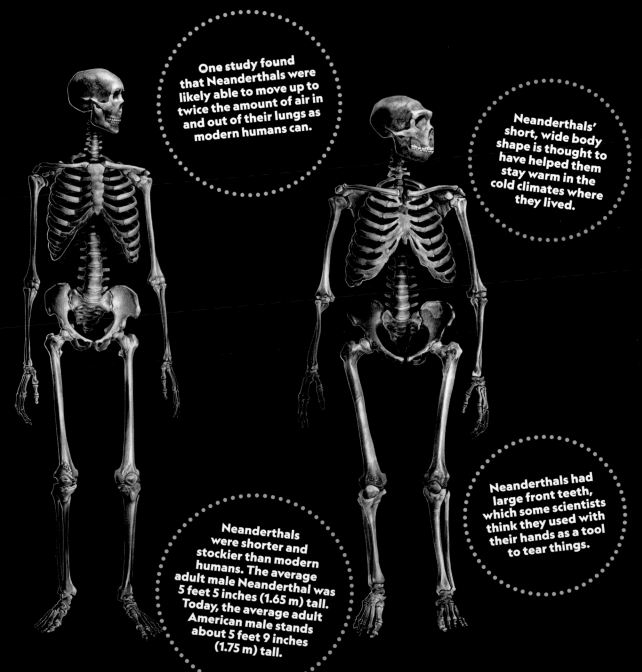

One study found that Neanderthals were likely able to move up to twice the amount of air in and out of their lungs as modern humans can.

Neanderthals' short, wide body shape is thought to have helped them stay warm in the cold climates where they lived.

Neanderthals were shorter and stockier than modern humans. The average adult male Neanderthal was 5 feet 5 inches (1.65 m) tall. Today, the average adult American male stands about 5 feet 9 inches (1.75 m) tall.

Neanderthals had large front teeth, which some scientists think they used with their hands as a tool to tear things.

# STEPHANIE GROCKE

Quetzaltenango (also known by its Maya name, Xela), Guatemala

## VOLCANOLOGIST

A volcanologist is a type of geologist—a scientist who studies rocks and minerals. Many types of igneous rocks are forged through volcanic activity. Volcanologists study these rocks and try to figure out how different kinds of volcanoes form and erupt.

**G**rowing up in Ohio, U.S.A., Dr. Stephanie Grocke loved the outdoors. But more than that, she was incredibly curious about the natural world.

"I wanted to know why there was a mountain where there was a mountain, and why there was a river where there was a river," she says.

She loved exploring and hiking in the woods and along the winding rivers that surrounded her home. When she traveled to the beach with her family, she would collect a cooler full of rocks and then lay them out on the ground to observe the differences between them.

In college, Stephanie began studying planet Earth and how it works through classes in geology. When one of her professors realized her interest in volcanoes, he encouraged her to do a summer program in Hawaii, during which she would study and live on the (active!) Kilauea volcano. It was there that she first witnessed a volcano erupting—an event that changed her life. As she watched bright red lava flow into the ocean against the pitch-dark night, that was it—she was hooked!

Making a career out of being near active volcanoes requires more than a little courage. One of Stephanie's first expeditions after graduate school was to Guatemala, with a group of more than 40

other scientists, to visit Santa María Volcano, potentially one of the most dangerous in the world, given its proximity to the more than one million people who live near it. Stephanie and the other scientists were there to test and compare a variety of techniques used to observe the volcano as it erupted. The goal? To get better at forecasting exactly when and how a volcano will erupt, so that people who live nearby can make evacuation plans and stay safe. But because most volcanic activity goes on deep in Earth's interior, eruptions are difficult to predict.

After that first trip to Santa María, Stephanie was eager to return. She wanted to discover and share more of this captivating volcano's story.

On her next trip, Stephanie used a type of 3D, time-lapse photography called photogrammetry to do a more in-depth study of the volcano. She used this technique to record one specific lava dome, called Santiaguito, which has been erupting pretty regularly for many years.

"It's difficult to see it with the naked eye," Stephanie says, "but Santiaguito is constantly changing. It's an evolving, dynamic system. Time-lapse photography lets us see that better."

To complete her mission, Stephanie needed a special team. "This trip wasn't going to

> **"**
> I wanted to know why there was a mountain where there was a mountain, and why there was a river where there was a river.
> **"**

be just about data collection," she says, "it was about telling the story of the volcanoes, so people—in Guatemala and around the world—can get to know more about how and why eruptions happen." So Stephanie recruited a photographer and a mapmaker to accompany her.

To get the images, Stephanie and her crew needed to set up three cameras near the summit of Santa María. They hauled their heavy camera equipment—as well as food, water, and camping gear—up a steep, narrow trail, all the way from the damp, thickly forested base of the mountain to the bare, windy top.

"When you get to the top of the volcano, you are completely exposed to the elements," Stephanie says. "It can be an entirely different weather pattern up there, and in our case, it was extremely windy and stormy. We had also just climbed about 4,000 feet (1,220 m), so we were dealing with the altitude and being totally exposed on the top of a barren summit."

The team got to work. First, Stephanie and the others focused their cameras on one of the erupting lava domes below. Stephanie set up a transmitter that could operate the cameras remotely, and they took photos simultaneously every few minutes. The team worked together for nearly five days to get their photos—waiting patiently when clouds and fog blocked their view. They endured the cold, rain, and wind. Afterward, they combined all the photos from the three cameras into a time-lapse video.

"These images will allow us to spot patterns of behavior that typically come before an eruption," Stephanie says. "We hope that, based on the patterns we recorded, we'll eventually get better at forecasting when an eruption is going to occur, and how bad that eruption will be."

Meanwhile, Stephanie and her team worked with staff members from the Instituto Gautemalteco de Turismo (INGUAT) in Quetzaltenango to create a public exhibit. They chose the best of their photos, captioned them, and made maps to show the locations of the active volcanic areas. They titled the exhibit "Viviendo con Volcanes," or "Living With Volcanoes." Stephanie hopes that seeing and hearing the story of the beautiful, dramatic volcanoes will deepen people's love of these unique environments—and help the people who live near them stay safe when eruptions do occur.

## STEPHANIE'S MUST-HAVE

A hand lens. As a geologist, she always has hers with her. She uses it to investigate rocks on a more magnified scale.

## PICTURE PERFECT

Scientists use photogrammetry to get precise measurements of landscapes and other three-dimensional (3D) objects. By combining photographs taken on multiple cameras from multiple viewpoints, they can create a 3D image of an object that can be used to measure distances between points on that object. Photogrammetry can also be used in combination with time-lapse photography to measure how points, or features, on an object move over time.

Lava domes form when magma wells up underground and erupts through a vent slowly, in the form of thick, sticky lava, which piles up and hardens in a dome shape around the vent.

## INSPIRATION STATION
### Stephanie's Advice for Aspiring Volcanologists

"Volcanoes are windows into the interior of our planet. There is so much we don't know about them and so much we can learn about our planet from them. Beyond volcanoes as a hazard, they hold many secrets about how our planet works. There's a lot of work to be done, so don't be discouraged. Go out there and delve into the unknown!"

71

# 3...2...1...

# VOLATILE, VARIED VOLCANOES

When a volcano erupts in a blaze of lava-flinging glory, it is the result of a process that has long been brewing beneath the planet's surface. This process begins with hot, melted rock deep below the surface, called magma. Magma pushes through the weak spots or cracks in the thick, rocky shell that surrounds Earth. When a crack extends all the way to the surface, pressure is suddenly released, and the volcano erupts!

## Let's take a look at a few kinds of volcanoes and their unique, awe-inspiring eruptions.

## LAVA DOME

Lava domes can produce the scariest and most destructive eruptions of all. When a vent becomes clogged with thick, sticky lava, magma builds up underneath, creating a bulgy dome-like shape. The eventual explosion, when it happens, can be extreme—shooting huge amounts of volcanic ash and gases into the air— and turning the surrounding rocks into rubble. All the material that shoots upward eventually comes tumbling down, in what volcanologists call a pyroclastic flow.

# ERUPT!

## STRATOVOLCANO

A stratovolcano may at certain times have huge, explosive eruptions, with dangerous pyroclastic flows. At other times it may erupt more quietly, with thinner lava pouring down its sides out of various cracks, or vents.

## SHIELD VOLCANO

This volcano forms when relatively thin, runny lava pours out over the ground during an eruption. Each eruption adds a layer, slowly building the volcano up into its wide, slightly mounded shape.

## CINDER CONE

It's the iconic, picture-book volcano: a cone with a dish-like crater at the top. Cinder cones form when volcanic ash shoots up out of a crack, or vent, in the ground and then settles around it.

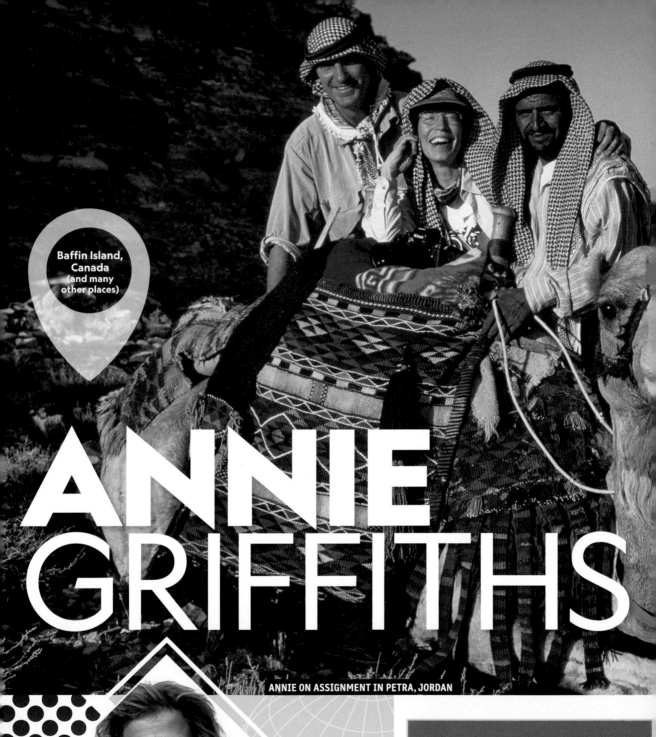

Baffin Island, Canada (and many other places)

# ANNIE GRIFFITHS

**ANNIE ON ASSIGNMENT IN PETRA, JORDAN**

## PHOTOGRAPHER

A photographer is someone who takes photographs to visually capture a moment, tell a story, and/or report the news.

I t was the late 1970s, and Annie Griffiths had just graduated college a year earlier and was working as a photographer for the *Worthington Daily Globe*, a regional newspaper in Minnesota, U.S.A. One day, she was developing photographs in the newspaper's darkroom when the phone rang. When she answered, a grumpy-sounding man asked, "Are you a photographer?" She said she was, and he replied, "I heard you had a heck of a hailstorm last night."

"Yes, sir, we did," Annie said, thinking maybe he was a local farmer.

"This is Bob Gilka at National Geographic," he said. "How fast can you get me a picture?"

Annie quickly sent Bob, who was the director of photography, a photo from the unusual weather event they'd had the night before, and to her delight, he published it!

While this exciting turn of events didn't immediately change Annie's life, it did give her the courage and the confidence to take the chance that did. About a year after that phone call, Annie sent her portfolio to Bob, along with a story pitch, an idea she had to photograph a canoe trip in Baffin Island, Canada.

Even though one of the other editors questioned whether Annie had enough experience, they ended up taking a chance and gave her the assignment. "Gilka called me up and said, 'Okay, go!'" she says. And that was it! Annie quit her job and embarked on what would be her first of many adventures with National Geographic.

Annie was one of the first female photographers at National Geographic, and while she was in the minority in her field and at the organization, she recognized quickly that her difference was also her strength. The fact that she was in territory that was relatively uncharted by women meant that she had a unique voice and a new perspective.

"Being one of the only women gave me the opportunity to tell stories that the guys often didn't know about or weren't able to tell," Annie says. She began looking more closely at stories that weren't being

> " Being one of the only women gave me the opportunity to tell stories that the guys often didn't know about or weren't able to tell. "

told, and she found that those stories were almost always about women. "There were just fewer photographers who were women and who could relate to women's everyday lives, who could understand where the heart of the story was, and who could earn the women's trust to tell it."

Annie was no stranger to trailblazing women. She grew up with a mother who broke barriers in her own right. From the time Annie's mom was little, she always had a fascination with and love of flying. In the 1940s, when she became old enough to work, she was told by an airline that it wouldn't hire her as a flight attendant because she wore glasses. So she said "Fine"—and became a pilot instead.

Annie, though, wasn't just one of the first women photographers on staff: She was the youngest person by far. "I was terrified," she says. Annie realized that the only way to combat her nagging fear that maybe she wasn't ready, or that maybe she wasn't good enough, was to work really hard. And that's exactly what she did. "I worked really long days. I did copious research. I tried to give the job everything I had. I was doing then what I still do now—earning the right to do important work. I earned that by giving 100 percent and by recognizing that I had a lot to learn." To date, Annie has worked on assignments in nearly 150 countries as a photographer for National Geographic.

Later, when Annie had two children, Lily and Charlie, she was again in a situation that not many of her male colleagues could relate to. It was during this time period in the United States—for the first time ever in history—that a majority of mothers continued to work after having children. Annie knew she could be a great mom and a great photographer—especially if she could do both at the same time. So she began pitching family-friendly stories and taking her kids with her. "Kids are fabulous travelers," she says. She never told anyone what she was doing, nor did she see any reason she should. She remembers thinking, *None of the guys I work with discuss their childcare situations, why should I?*

It wasn't long before Lily and Charlie knew exactly what their globe-trotting adventures were all about—finding cool pictures. "I remember a time when Lily was six or seven years old," Annie says. "We were doing a story on Sydney, Australia,

and she came running into the little apartment where we were living and said, 'Mommy come quickly, they're doing the most wonderful thing on the beach!'" Annie ran down to find a group of locals making a serpentine piece of art that stretched all the way down the shoreline. Lily was right, it made a great picture. So great, in fact, that it was published as part of the story in *National Geographic* magazine.

While Annie, Lily, and Charlie had many adventures of a lifetime, there were definitely ordinary moments, too, like long, boring car rides. On assignment for a story about Badlands National Park and Custer State Park in South Dakota, U.S.A., they listened to kids books on tape while they drove down endless stretches of highway. And there were certainly early mornings, like the time they were on a shoot in Arizona and—to get the best light—Annie, Lily, and Charlie would have to leave the hotel at four in the morning.

"I'd have to roll them out of bed, put them in the car, and fasten their seat belts, all while they were fast asleep," Annie says. She'd have blankets and pillows for them while they slept, and fruit and doughnuts for them when they woke up. When Annie arrived at the shoot location, she'd get out and begin taking photographs, and the kids had strict instructions to stay in the car. When they woke up, they knew to roll down the window and call out to her. "We did that day after day," she says, "and they never complained."

For about five years, from the time Lily was five years old and Charlie was two, Annie often worked on assignments in the Middle East. Once, she and her children spent a long time with a group of women living near the border of Saudi Arabia. "There were so many aspects of who I was that [the women] couldn't relate to," she says. "We didn't share a language, we dressed differently, they could not imagine traveling by themselves to a different country, but I didn't seem completely alien or unrelatable to them because I had these two little kids to take care of."

Before long, all the kids were playing together in the dirt, as kids from every corner of the world do. "You know, we build bridges in funny ways," Annie says, "and the mere fact of being a woman has opened a lot of doors for me."

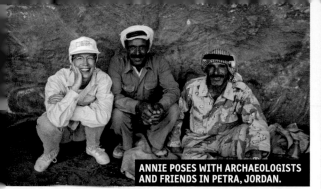

ANNIE POSES WITH ARCHAEOLOGISTS AND FRIENDS IN PETRA, JORDAN.

HIKERS TREK THROUGH FIORDLAND NATIONAL PARK, NEW ZEALAND, IN THIS PHOTO TAKEN BY ANNIE.

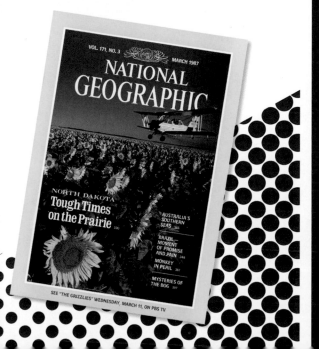

# ANNIE'S TIPS FOR ASPIRING PHOTOGRAPHERS

**1) Shoot more. Plan less.** The worst thing you can do is sit inside thinking, *Should I go shoot the soccer game or should I not?* Just go outside with your camera, with no plan, and shoot what you see. And try not to overthink things like light, movement, and composition. Just pick up your camera and start taking pictures.

**2) Tell a story.** If you're photographing the tennis team, don't worry about the game—tell the story of the players. If you're going to cover a parade, don't just go to the parade itself. Get there early, while the bands are getting ready, and then stay afterward, when everybody's worn out. If you're shooting a play, you want to be backstage with people when they're tired and when they're excited. You want to see the experience through their eyes.

**3) Be in the moment.** Don't think about what taking a great picture might lead to—like an art show, an A+ in the class, or a scholarship—instead, get lost in the story you're telling. If you love photography, think: *What can you photograph right now?*

**4) Go further.** Don't just take one picture and think, *That's it!* Instead, think, *OK! Now what else can I do?* Maybe you took a really great picture of the bench at the baseball game, and then one of all the players on the bench watching the game. Maybe next you should shoot some of the details, like the bat and ball.

**5) Be curious.** Ask questions and be curious about the answers. Continuing the baseball example, ask what the players' superstitions are and if they have any traditions. Do they get together and do a cheer? Shoot that. Does every player touch first base when they take the field? If so, then lay your body down at first base and show a foot running by it, touching first base. Tell that story.

Hwange National Park, Zimbabwe

# MOREANGELS MBIZAH

It was the dry season in Hwange National Park. Dr. Moreangels Mbizah and two of her research assistants had been tracking a pride of lions for several days. Late one afternoon, they spotted the lions asleep under a tree in an open, grassy area. Then, as they watched from the safety of their Land Cruiser, something extraordinary happened. Several African buffalo walked past, on their way to a nearby water hole. The lions immediately became alert and then started chasing the buffalo.

Moreangels had studied lions in the field for many seasons. She had collected tons of data about how lion prides feed, what they feed on, and how changes in their prey populations can change the lions' behavior and their own interactions. But in all those seasons, she had never seen a successful hunt happen right before her eyes. That was about to change.

"It was beautiful to watch the coordination between the lions as they brought one of the buffalo down," she says, "and it was so interesting to see that the hunters were all females. The male was just there watching, not participating in the hunt."

The main goal of Moreangels's research is to identify threats to lions, such as the loss of their prey populations or other changes in their habitat, and to find innovative ways of addressing these threats. Lions are very shy, they sleep for much of the day, and most of their hunting is done at night. It can be difficult to get even a glimpse of them in the wild. To track them and find them more easily, researchers will fit at least one of the lions in a pride with a collar that holds a special GPS device. On their computers or smartphones, they can connect to the GPS signal. And the data from the GPS allow them to map the lions' general location and keep track of their movements over time. When they notice a pride staying in one area for several hours, it may indicate that the lions have recently killed prey and are feeding there. Then, Moreangels and her crew drive to that location to observe and collect the data they need.

If a lion hasn't moved for a while, it could also mean that it has been injured or snared. In that case, the researchers will check to see if the animal is OK. And if it has been hurt, they can treat its injuries. That's why GPS tracking is really important: not only for the data it provides, but also for protecting the lions themselves.

That was the case with Cecil, one of the lions that Moreangels was studying. He was a big favorite among park visitors, who were sometimes lucky enough to spot him playing with the cubs in his large pride. On July 6, 2015, one of the research assistants did a routine check of all the GPS downloads, and he noticed something wrong. Cecil's GPS collar had not been transmitting data for two days. "That got everyone worried," Moreangels says. At first, they thought maybe the collar's battery had died. But the next day, park rangers heard a rumor that a lion had

> " As long as there is something that I can contribute toward conservation, then that is worth fighting for. "

79

been shot, just outside the park. Could it have been Cecil? Even more worried, a researcher and park ranger got in the Land Cruiser and drove toward Cecil's last known location. When they got there, their fears were confirmed. It was Cecil, and he had been shot. There was nothing they could do to help him.

Hunting is illegal throughout Hwange National Park, but big-game hunters had lured him outside the park boundary with elephant meat, and they'd shot him with a bow and arrow. Cecil was dead, and his head and skin had been taken as a trophy.

Lions once flourished throughout the grasslands and savannas of Africa, but today, because of human activities such as hunting and habitat destruction, there are only a few scattered populations left. Most of these are confined to park lands, and their numbers are dwindling rapidly. Without protection from humans, lions could soon vanish from the world forever. Moreangels tries to think about what might have been learned from the heartbreaking situation with Cecil.

"It opened many people's eyes to conservation issues," she says. "When Cecil died, there was a lot of media attention, and there was soon a global outcry against trophy hunting. So although losing Cecil was a terrible thing, the good thing that came out of it was that more people started paying attention." Thousands of people made donations, and researchers were able to use that money to buy new tracking equipment and to employ more lion guardians from the local communities.

Conservation research can sometimes feel overwhelming. It can be difficult to not get discouraged when there's news of another animal becoming endangered or extinct, and to wonder if the work you're doing is having an impact. "Thinking about the end results of my efforts always keeps me going," Moreangels says. "It's going to be small. But as long as there is an impact, as long as there is something that I can contribute toward conservation, then that is worth fighting for."

Around the world, many people are working hard to stop lions from disappearing. Moreangels is concerned that very few of those people come from the countries that are most affected by the loss, such as Zimbabwe. She believes the communities that live with the lions are the ones best suited to help them. But for people to care about the fate of these animals, they must first be exposed to them, and get a chance to see them and learn about how wildlife preservation can actually make their own lives better. "I think of my childhood in Zimbabwe," she says. "The first time I saw a wild animal was when I was 25 years old, even though lions and African wild dogs lived just a few miles from my home. Perhaps if we'd had the chance to interact with wildlife when we were children, more of my classmates would be working alongside me now."

The work that Moreangels does to conserve unique and important animals, like Cecil, is so significant, and it doesn't come without sacrifice. Moreangels has studied lions in the field for many seasons, constantly traveling between her field site and her son in another country. Where Moreangels is from, it's difficult for her, as a woman and a mother, to leave for months at a time to study in Hwange National Park. There is a double standard—men may pursue a career far from their spouse or children without being judged or criticized, but for women, Moreangels says, the same actions are often seen as unacceptable.

"But it is something that I love," she says, "so I have to find a way." As a role model and mentor—especially for young women and African conservationists—Moreangels wants to make sure that environmental studies become part of every African child's education, so that the future can be brighter for everyone—people and animals included.

## INSPIRATION STATION
### Moreangels's Advice for Aspiring Conservation Biologists

"My advice is to talk to people already in the field and find a good mentor. Look for good role models for inspiration, too, because sometimes it will get tough. But when you have people who inspire you, that will help you carry on. Also, try to volunteer with conservation projects to get to know more about wildlife. That will give you valuable experience and help you decide which kind of conservation you want to focus on."

# STRAIGHT FROM THE SCIENTIST

**Are you often the only woman out in the field when you're working on these lion study projects?**

"Yes, and it's sometimes difficult to be the only woman among all the men, but they treat me as an equal and respect me as a person, and I think that's why we work together very well. It's not common in Zimbabwe, or in most African countries, for women to be field scientists. When I meet young girls in the local villages, they get very excited to see me doing fieldwork."

## 📖 MOREANGELS'S READING REC

*The African Wild Dog: Behavior, Ecology, and Conservation* by Scott Creel and Nancy Marusha Creel. "When I first began working in conservation, it got me very interested," Moreangels says. "I learned that the African wild dog is endangered and that there are many factors causing its decline, including competition with other large carnivores. This book really inspired me to get more involved in wildlife conservation, and particularly in how predator and prey interact."

A lion's diet can include zebras, giraffes, warthogs, and impalas. In Hwange, the lions' favorite food is buffalo.

# High-Tech

## Saving Lions With Conservation Tech

Researchers like Moreangels use some pretty high-tech tools to keep tabs on lions—the second largest big cat species in the world (just behind tigers). Over the past 25 years, it's estimated that the African lion population has decreased by half. In an effort to try to learn as much as they can about lions, their behavior, and the threats they face, animal conservationists keep track of individual lions and their prides to study and observe them. To do this, they use various types of technology. Here are a few.

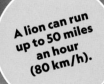

A lion can run up to 50 miles an hour (80 km/h).

### Geofencing

Sometimes people harm lions because they feel like the animals are dangerous. And farmers might hurt lions if their livestock has been killed and eaten by lions. Conservationists can prevent these negative interactions using geofencing, an electronic barrier between areas where wildlife roam and communities where humans live. If a lion crosses that barrier, an alert is sent via text to someone who can alert community members that a lion is approaching. Then, villagers can get to a safe place and farmers can move their animals into a safe enclosure.

# Helpers

A lion may sleep up to 20 hours a day!

## GPS Tracking Collar

Once a selected lion is sedated, it is fitted with a collar that contains a GPS tracking device, which detects and records its exact location. This information is then used by scientists and conservationists. It helps them learn more about lion behavior and movements—for example, when a pride merges with other prides, and then later when it separates into smaller groups. The device also lets them to know when a lion has stopped moving, indicating that it could be hurt, sick, or in a trap set by hunters.

A lion's roar is so loud it can be heard up to five miles (8 km) away!

## Acoustic Sensor

A lion's roar tells scientists and conservationists a lot about the animal's behavior. To hear the roars—and learn which lion is making the sound, and when, how loud, and for how long it roars—an acoustic sensor is placed on the lion's GPS collar and records the sounds made by the lion and the nearby members of its pride.

## LONG-DISTANCE HIKER

Long-distance hikers train to increase their endurance, backpacking, and outdoor safety skills, in preparation for walking many miles in rugged conditions, usually in wilderness areas.

Appalachian Trail, U.S.A.

# JENNIFER PHARR DAVIS

After graduating from college, Jennifer had no idea what to do with her life.

But she felt a strong yearning, for the first time, to get out into nature. "My entire education had happened inside classrooms," she says. "I didn't know the difference between an oak tree or a maple. I was so out of touch with the natural environment."

Jennifer had heard a lot of stories about the Appalachian Trail (or A.T.). It had challenged generations of long-distance hikers, and it seemed like just the place for Jennifer to reflect on her life, and her future.

She guessed hiking the entire trail couldn't be that difficult. After all, she'd played sports all her life. *And hiking was really just walking,* she thought. *So, how hard could it be?*

She learned pretty quickly—it can be really hard. On her second day on the trail, her legs were so tired they shook every time she walked downhill. She once broke her camp stove after dropping it into a hot pot of mac and cheese. And trying to drive her tent stakes into the frozen ground, at night, in the dark, left her sleeping under a collapsed tent on more than a couple occasions. "I got out there and, yeah, I got it handed to me,"

> **"**
> I was literally hiking down mountains backward because that was the only way I could keep going.
> **"**

she says. "I was so humbled by the trail." But she completed the entire A.T., and as she met each challenge on her own, her self-confidence grew.

The Appalachian Trail has challenged hikers for generations. It is the longest marked hiking trail in the world, stretching through 14 states, from Mount Katahdin in central Maine down to Springer Mountain in northern Georgia. A.T. hikers trek through open meadows and deep woods. They scramble over steep mountains and rocky outcrops and cross high ridges with breathtaking views. For many, hiking just one stretch of the A.T. is a lifetime goal. Jennifer is among a smaller group of thru-hikers—people who have successfully walked the entire length of the 2,180-mile (3,508-km) trail within one season.

After that life-changing first hike, Jennifer didn't think she'd ever get the opportunity to hike another long trail. She found a job at a museum, and she got on with her life. But she missed being out in nature, the adventure, and how she felt on the trail. On the A.T., with no showers, limited hygiene products, and lots of dirt and bugs and sweat, she felt beautiful. "I saw myself through my interactions with other hikers," Jennifer says. "If I was kind, or funny, or could make someone smile, they became my reflection, and that made me feel pretty. I began to base my self-worth on what I could do, not how I looked." It wasn't long before Jennifer felt the itch of the trail, and headed out for more.

She worked hard, saved her money, and took hiking trips to places like Kilimanjaro and Machu Picchu whenever she could get time away from work. Then, Jennifer decided to give the A.T. a second try—this time shooting for the women's record for speed. She had recently gotten married, and her husband agreed to help her, meeting her at crossroads along the way with food and supplies.

It was a success: Jennifer completed the trail in 57 days, shattering the previous women's record of 99 days. But, with a mere 10 days between Jennifer's record and the fastest record set by a man, she felt as if she could do more. "I felt I could have beaten that record, if I'd started with the right mindset," she says. "If I'd only said to myself, 'I'm a competitor. I'm going for the overall record,' rather than 'I'm a female. I can't compete with the guys.'" She knew she had to try the trail again.

Three years later, Jennifer began her third hike of the A.T., with the goal of breaking the overall speed record, not just the women's record. She began in mid-June at Mount Katahdin with high hopes, but within just a few days, she felt like the whole trip was falling apart. First, she got painful, crippling shin splints. "I was literally hiking down mountains backward," she says, "because that was the only way I could keep going."

Then, when she arrived at Franconia Ridge in New Hampshire, already behind schedule, a ferocious rainstorm moved in and stayed for more than 24 hours. As she climbed higher, the rain turned to sleet. The high wind blew icy needles against her skin and through her clothing, chilling her to the bone. The visibility was so low, all she could see were the rocks beneath her feet. She tried to sing her favorite songs, to keep herself going, but she became so fuzzy-headed from the cold, she couldn't even remember the words. "I said to myself, 'Just keep walking,'" she says. She knew if she stopped, she was more likely to get hypothermia, a sometimes life-threatening condition in which the body begins losing more heat than it can make.

As on the previous hike, she planned to meet her husband and her small support crew each day at assigned crossroads. On this day, her husband had become worried that she could be suffering from hypothermia, so he hiked into the woods to meet her on the trail, set up a tent, brought her dry clothes, fed her, and wrapped her in two sleeping bags to warm her up. That gave her the strength to keep going, but barely.

"The next day was super hard," Jennifer remembers. "The start of hypothermia had taken a lot out of me. I somehow made it into Vermont, but then I became very, very sick. I'd never felt so bad in my

entire life." As she stumbled out of the woods at their meeting place, she told her husband, "I quit. I'm done. Take me home."

He looked at her and told her that if she wanted to quit, fine, but he wanted her to wait until she felt a bit better to make that decision. "Keep going until tomorrow night," he said. "If you still want to quit then, I'll take you home." He dropped off her provisions and drove away. Soon the medicine he'd brought her began to kick in, and she was able to eat a little food and drink some water. By the next evening, just as her husband had thought, she no longer wanted to quit.

Nevertheless, she was so far behind where she wanted to be, the speed record now seemed way out of reach. And to make matters worse, she still felt weak and woozy. "So, I decided to just keep going—not to set the record—but to find my personal best," she says. As soon as she took that pressure off, she began enjoying herself and clocking miles. In a few days, Jennifer was actually back on pace to set the record.

On July 30, 2011, in the early afternoon, surrounded by cheering friends and family, Jennifer reached the end of the trail at Springer Mountain once again. She and her crew knew they had done it. It had been a long and extremely challenging journey, but taking it one day at a time, they had indeed set the overall record. She walked 2,180 miles (3,508 km) in 46 days, 11 hours, and 20 minutes. That's an average of 47 miles (75.5 km) a day—nearly the distance of two marathons! Until that day, no woman or man had done it faster. But for Jennifer, the greatest victory is that her story inspires other people to spend time outside. "It doesn't matter what their goal is, whether they want to set a record or just spend a night in the woods," she says. "That's the real joy."

Jennifer has hiked more than 14,000 miles (22,500 km) of long-distance trails, in all 50 states and across six different continents.

## WHAT'S THE BEST THRU-HIKE FOOD?

Food you don't have to chew! Jennifer needed to consume 6,000 to 7,000 calories a day to stay healthy and energetic on her hike. That's a lot of eating. By the end of the day, she was so tired, she wanted high-calorie food that would give her energy and didn't require a ton of effort to eat. One of her favorite trail snacks was a new take on a traditional peanut butter and jelly sandwich, made with Pop-Tarts instead of bread. Voilà! An 800-calorie peanut butter sandwich.

# TRAIL TRIUMPH
## How Pros Prepare for a Thru-Hike

When hiking for days or weeks to complete a trail, preparation is the name of the game. Thru-hikers aim to make sure they have what they'll need for the various situations they might encounter, but they have to be careful not to overpack. Because don't forget: They have to carry everything. On their back. For weeks in the wilderness.

Test the gear. Experienced thru-hikers take everything they plan to use on their hike out for a test run. If the way a new backpack sits on their hips feels uncomfortable or painful after two *miles* (3.2 km), imagine how it will feel after two *weeks*.

Train. Before thru-hikers embark on their multiweek trip, they get their bodies prepared. This involves lots of day hikes, on varying terrains, while wearing their pack and the shoes they plan to bring.

Break in new shoes. In everyday life, blisters are a bummer. On long hikes, though, blisters can be brutal (and sometimes even adventure-ending) for hikers. So thru-hikers make sure they have great shoes and that they break them in properly.

Get a water filter. When on a long hike, one or two water bottles won't be enough. So hikers carry a light water filter with them because even fresh running streams can carry microbes that can make people sick.

Do food math! Hikers estimate how many calories they will burn while they hike, so that they know how much they should eat to replenish them. Because hiking burns lots of calories, high-impact snacks like nuts, coconut, chocolate, and peanut butter are a must!

Set small goals. Even seasoned thru-hikers can become overwhelmed by an endless-seeming journey. So when they begin their trek, they break up the distance into smaller chunks, thinking about where they'll stop for the night, or the next time they'll travel through a town.

# MALLORY DIMMITT

## EXPEDITION LEADER

An expedition leader is in charge of planning and organizing an outdoor journey, often with specific goals such as collecting data, exploring a lesser known route, or raising public awareness about a particular area.

**Florida Wildlife Corridor, U.S.A.**

The state of Florida is a wildlife-lover's dream. The peninsula is surrounded by waters teeming with manatees, turtles, dolphins, and sharks. On land, it's home to unique environments like the marshy Florida Everglades as well as species such as panthers, black bears, indigo snakes, and more. But Florida's human population has been growing fast. Where there were seven million people just 50 years ago, today there are more than 21 million. Houses, highways, shopping centers, and golf courses are springing up everywhere—in places where wild animals used to live.

Florida's wild land is shrinking. To make matters worse, the remaining wildlife habitats are often left broken up into small, isolated pieces, separated by human-occupied spaces. This is called habitat fragmentation. When this happens, animals can become isolated from other animals like them, making it hard for them to reproduce. Habitat fragmentation is one of the main causes of stress on wildlife, and it can ultimately lead to species becoming endangered or extinct.

Mallory Dimmitt's goal is to protect and restore Florida's wildlife habitats, and to connect them to one another so that animals have an uninterrupted area to roam.

"The first step in saving these habitats," Mallory says, "is to open people's eyes to the amazing wild lands that are hiding in plain sight—right in their own backyard." Mallory hopes that people will want to protect them. She and her team from the Florida Wildlife Corridor organization complete both long and short expeditions through Florida's wild lands and share the photos and video footage with the public. Their first expedition covered 1,000 miles (1,600 km)—from Everglades National Park at the southern tip of Florida to the Okefenokee National Wildlife Refuge in southern Georgia. It took them 100 days! Mallory and three colleagues—a wildlife biologist, a photojournalist, and a filmmaker—hiked, paddled, biked, and swam the entire length of the state. Together they watched wildlife, took amazing pictures of the nature they saw, wrote about their challenges, and produced an incredible hour-long film about their adventure when they were done.

That first expedition was such a rush that Mallory signed on for the job of planning and leading the next. As director of the "Glades to Gulf" trek in 2015,

Mallory was in charge of organizing and executing another 1,000-mile (1,600-km) hike—from the headwaters of the Everglades west through Florida's Panhandle. "We hike through the same areas that wildlife would actually travel, and use the paths they would use," Mallory says. Along the way, Mallory and her team posted updates about their progress on social media. Afterward, they produced an hour-long video to tell the story of their journey into the wilderness and to capture people's imaginations.

Today, Mallory continues to lead expeditions in Florida, but instead of a huge expedition every few years, the Florida Wildlife Corridor organization does a shorter, one-week trip every year.

"Our hope is to keep reinspiring our [social media] followers and get new people involved every year," Mallory says. For these trips, Mallory and her team moves along the edges of urban areas, through the parts of the corridor that are most at risk of being cut off or lost. Their first seven-day trip began at the Disney Wilderness Preserve, south of the city of Orlando. Most people visiting Walt Disney World probably don't even know that, just beyond the park's various attractions and rides, there are significant acres of wild land.

"Surrounding the theme parks are forests, natural areas, and creeks," she says. "And Disney does a good job of managing these areas and keeping them wild."

Mallory and her team picked one creek corridor to travel along—a creek that winds its way right through the heart of Disney World. They didn't see any of the rides or theme parks as they paddled along in their canoes. But in the distance, they could hear the noise, and even the loudspeaker in the parking areas, directing people where to go. "It felt so strange to be in a relatively wild place, yet close to thousands of people on both sides."

Mallory and her team wanted to experience for themselves exactly what wild animals experience as they move through this fragmented habitat. A number of major highways all converge on Disney World, and trying to get across busy highways can be a big problem for migrating wildlife. Special wildlife crossings that go under the highways help animals navigate more safely. Several times, Mallory and her team had to paddle through these underpasses. They could hear the traffic whizzing overhead. At one point, much to the surprise of some wide-eyed golfers, the creek took them right through the middle of a golf course. It was quite a surprise for them to see a wilderness expedition canoeing through the manicured waterway.

Just outside the theme-park area, the paddling became challenging, and the team slogged through shallow swampy stretches and waters clogged with duckweed, a type of flowering aquatic plant. "It was tough going for us, but a great place for wildlife," Mallory says. "It was early spring, so everything in this beautiful forest was a vibrant, bright green, and we had a lot of wildlife encounters." They saw water snakes, an otter, a barred owl. Then, as they were paddling around a curve in the creek, they came to a stop: A long-legged wading bird, a limpkin, was having a buffet of freshwater clams. Instead of flying off, it continued on, carrying the clams over to the riverbank one by one, and then eating them. It wasn't at all afraid of Mallory and her crew. They were in awe.

Mallory's expeditions have shown her how resilient nature can be, and how closely wild animals can live to human-built environments. But wild corridors are essential. If they are broken, Florida's wilderness could be lost forever. As Mallory and her team left the creek and began to hike west toward their goal—the Green Swamp Wilderness Preserve—they stopped to camp in the cabins at Lake Louisa State Park. Here, on a high ridge overlooking the lake, they invited other conservationists, land managers, and scientists to join them.

Sitting around the campfire under the big starry sky, everyone shared their stories. "We wanted to hear what they were working on, what they were most proud of, their successes and challenges," Mallory says. She hopes that the people who see their photographs and films and read the blogs and books about their expeditions will be inspired to join this growing group of dedicated Floridians working to preserve the state's wild places.

> " We hike through the same areas that wildlife would actually travel, and use the paths they would use. "

# INSPIRATION STATION
## Mallory's Advice for Aspiring Adventurers

"Pursue your passions. My first passion was kayaking, and I learned to white-water paddle at summer camp. I fell in love with that, and always kept working to take it to the next level. I started to plan paddling trips with friends. Even though they were just for fun, I got a lot of experience. The key is to cultivate your curiosity and seek out different people who will be great adventure buddies. Then you can practice and develop your skills together and start exploring areas you've never been to, expedition style."

# STRAIGHT FROM THE SCIENTIST
## How do you sleep in a swamp?

"We mostly sleep in hammocks, with mesh screens for mosquito control. When we started our third trip, the weather was chilly, and we were a little more exposed in a hammock than we would have been in a tent, so my back got cold. But then by the end of the trip it was hot, and when you're hot and sticky, sleeping in a hammock can be uncomfortably snug! I try to lie still and focus on listening to all the night noises I can distinguish until I fall asleep."

## MALLORY'S MUST-HAVE

Fun! Mallory and her team like to play along the way—they toss Frisbees between canoes and sometimes get out in the swamp to splash around and throw a football. Together they biked the final 25 miles (40 km) to the Green Swamp. When they got there, they jumped into the dark waters for a celebratory swim.

The Green Swamp is Florida's second largest wetland and forms the headwaters for four of Florida's central rivers.

# WHERE THE WILD THINGS GO
## MAPPING NORTH AMERICA'S WILDLIFE CORRIDORS

Today, all around the world, wild animals sometimes wander out of the woods or jungle or swamp where they live and into human-made spaces, like highways, backyards, or parking lots. As the wild lands occupied by animals shrink, both humans and animals are put in danger. That's where wildlife corridors come in. They are continuous stretches of land protected by humans to be used by wildlife. Here are a few found in North America.

## Yellowstone to Yukon

The Yellowstone to Yukon Conservation Initiative, nicknamed Y2Y, is an effort to connect nearly 2,000 miles (3,220 km) of wild lands and animal habitats stretching from Yellowstone National Park in the United States to the Yukon, a territory in northwest Canada. There are already more than 100 over- and underpasses to help wild animals safely cross busy roads. Some of the animals that the Y2Y wildlife corridor benefits are grizzly bears, bighorn sheep, elk, wolves, cougars, and deer.

## Burnham Wildlife Corridor

This 100-acre (40.5-ha) stretch of wilderness is located on the edge of a big, bustling city—Chicago, Illinois, U.S.A. The area is located along the lakefront and offers wild animals prairie, savanna, and woodland ecosystems, rich with native plant, shrub, and tree species. This stretch of protected wilderness gives migrating birds and butterflies a safe place to stop along their journey, and the land also filters water that flows into Lake Michigan, helping keep the lake cleaner.

## Florida Wildlife Corridor

The hope is that this corridor will connect 15.8 million acres (6.4 million ha) of wild lands and animal habits all around the state of Florida. The lands that the corridor will include are home to 42 endangered and 24 threatened species, including the green turtle, Everglades snail kite, frosted flatwoods salamander, Florida panther, and more.

# SANDHYA
## NARAYANAN

The border between Peru and Bolivia in South America

## LINGUISTIC ANTHROPOLOGIST
Someone who studies how the use of language and languages influence people and societies.

n the house where Dr. Sandhya Narayanan grew up, at any given time you could hear at least five different languages being spoken—Tamil, Malayalam, Hindi, Bengali, and English.

Sandhya spent part of her childhood in Toronto, Canada, and then part of it in Boston, Massachusetts, U.S.A. In both of these places, many of her neighbors were immigrants. With people from all over the world living in the same place, Sandhya's communities were full of many different languages and cultures, all the time.

Growing up, Sandhya knew that she was different from the other kids she went to school with and the other families in her neighborhood. Everyone in her neighborhood was vastly different from one another. They had different customs, different religions, different cuisines. But she also knew that she was different from her extended family back in India, as well.

"My family would visit India and I would interact with my cousins there," Sandhya says, "but I felt that I was also different than them. I spent a lot of my teenage years trying to figure out those differences."

Then, when Sandhya went to college, she began taking linguistics and anthropology courses. Linguistics is the study of languages, and anthropology is the study of humans, their societies, and their cultures. Through these courses, Sandhya found out that there were researchers studying something called multilingualism, which describes communities where multiple languages are spoken. Some anthropologists are interested in understanding how, in one place, there can be different languages and ways of speaking, and how these ways of speaking change and remain the same over time. Sandhya was floored! There were people who dedicated their careers to studying experiences similar to hers growing up.

"I found it to be one of those great ironies that people were going out and studying what I'd been living my entire life," she says. "It was the first time I really felt empowered about my own upbringing and experiences."

Sandhya began studying multilingualism. It was interesting and exciting, and she found it healing to learn more about people around the world who had similar experiences to her own. "Those classes showed me that, actually, there is something special about how I grew up and how I came to understand the world," she says.

Sandhya was so taken with the subject that she has made it her career. Today, she studies multilingualism in a region on the border between Peru and Bolivia, high up in the Andes mountain range, where the indigenous languages Quechua and Aymara are spoken. When there is more than one language being spoken in a community, Sandhya is interested in why—and in what specific situations—someone chooses to speak one language rather than another. Sometimes the reasons are political, sometimes they're practical, and sometimes they're deeply personal. "In my work, I investigate the differences in language across the world," Sandhya says, "but I also am interested in identifying the basic things that connect us to each other."

To get a better understanding of the languages the people in the region are speaking, and how they use them, Sandhya travels up through the surrounding mountains. Her journey starts at 12,400 feet (3,800 m) above sea level and climbs even higher. Some of the communities she studies are in the jungle, and to get there she has to take multiple cars, winding around sharp turns on super narrow streets. On one side are mountains, and on the other side? A steep drop-off.

"You are constantly thrown from one side of the car to the other," Sandhya says. "The first time I took one of these cars, the driver had all these plastic bags in the front, and I had no idea why. Then, after the first trip, I realized why. I never thought I had motion sickness until I went down to the jungle the first time … I threw up a lot."

Once she got there, though, it was beautiful. The community members grow crops such as cacao, coffee, oranges, and clementines. "In the jungle, the car goes slow enough that if you open up the window, you can reach out and grab a couple bananas or oranges along the way," Sandhya says. "That winding, hairpin-turn-filled nightmare is always worth it."

> 66
> It was the first time I really felt empowered about my own upbringing and experiences.
> 99

Sandhya has been working in and studying the same 10 or so villages for more than five years. For her research in this region, Sandhya spends a lot of time observing both the languages that individual people are speaking and how they speak them, the languages being spoken in public spaces, like at the market, in schools, and at various celebrations. When she studies individual people, she uses a voice recorder while she interviews them and asks them to tell her about themselves.

"I say things like, 'Tell me about your life. Tell me about your language. Tell me funny stories,'" Sandhya says. They can respond in whatever language they feel most comfortable speaking. That way, Sandhya can see how speaking patterns vary among people from different age groups, and different geographic and social backgrounds.

During these interviews, Sandhya will go along with her subject while they do whatever it is they would normally be doing. She's accompanied them to the marketplace, and she's interviewed others during downtime in the fields where they plant potatoes or quinoa. Some situations, she's learned, are more challenging than others. "Once, I was living in a village that had a donkey and it would hee-haw every hour, or when the weather changed," she says. "One day, I planned an interview near where the donkey was and I scheduled it for five minutes

TRADITIONAL INDIGENOUS DANCERS PARADE IN THE STREETS OF PUNO, PERU.

after I expected the donkey to hee-haw. But for some reason, the donkey wouldn't stop hee-hawing! It did it during my entire interview, and I ended up just having to reschedule."

A lot of the people Sandhya studies are from indigenous groups, which means they are descendants of the first people who ever inhabited the area. Some of them speak languages that are unique to their indigenous communities. For indigenous people who live in multilingual communities, it can be a difficult to decide whether to teach their language to their children. That's because their children might mainly speak a different language at school or at work or with their friends.

Some languages, therefore, are at risk of not being adopted by younger generations and, maybe, disappearing. But language is an enormous part of people's culture, heritage, and identity, which is something that Sandhya has known—and felt— since she was a little girl growing up in a busy household full of friends and family from all over the world. How someone chooses to speak, which language they choose to use, and when, is complicated, and it can be very personal and political. "I really get it," Sandhya says. "I understand the challenge, and I don't have an easy answer. That's why I research this, to figure out how people make those difficult decisions." Being able to connect her research to her own experiences growing up gives Sandhya a great sense of purpose and fulfillment, she says. "I feel like I am studying things that really do matter."

**SANDHYA CAPTURES A POST-RECORDING MOMENT OF SUCCESS IN THE FIELD.**

# INSPIRATION STATION
## Sandhya's Advice for Aspiring Anthropologists

"One: Think big. If you like imagining how people live and you are curious about that, then keep that curiosity and that imagination and that creativity. Two: Always take care of yourself and be aware of how best to do that. Three: Take measured risks, but don't be afraid to make mistakes. You're going to fail sometimes, but it's OK! Four: Always have a good sense of humor because it will get you through even not-so-great times."

# SANDHYA'S READING REC

*The Horse and His Boy* by C. S. Lewis. "It's about a cross-country horse trip through all of these different places with different languages," Sandhya says. "Ten-year-old Sandhya thought that it would never happen in real life. And now, I'm doing similar things, traveling around the world where people speak all sorts of languages."

**RESIDENTS OF PACCAJE, PERU, PARTAKE IN A CELEBRATION HONORING THEIR LOCAL MOUNTAIN DEITY.**

# The Life of a Language

Today, there are more than 7,000 different languages spoken around the world. Some are spoken by a lot of people, like Mandarin Chinese (917 million), Spanish (450 million), and English (1.5 billion). And some are spoken by many fewer people, like Quechua, one of the languages Sandhya studies, (8 million), or Jaqaru, a language spoken by about 700 people in Peru.

In fact, there are dozens of languages today that have only one native speaker still living. After that person dies, the language will become lost. More than 40 percent of the world's languages are endangered, which means they are at serious risk of being lost.

### How do we lose a language?

One common way this occurs is when there is pressure for people to speak a language other than their native language at school, work, and outside the home. Then, as younger generations only speak their native language at home, or perhaps don't ever learn to speak it at all, little by little, fewer people learn and speak that language, putting it in danger of extinction.

### What happens when a language is lost?

A language is a unique way of communication shared by a group of people. These words can express the specific foods, feelings, and traditions that a community share. When a language is lost, a certain record of a culture is lost, too.

## HOW TO SAY "HELLO!"
### Learn greetings from around the world and more about their languages of origin.

**ALOHA**
*(pronounced ah-LOH-hah)*

Language: Hawaiian
Where it's spoken: Hawaiian Islands
About how many native speakers: 8,000

**NAMASKARA**
*(pronounced nah-mas-KAR-ah)*

Language: Kannada
Where it's spoken: Kannada is the official language of the state of Karnataka in Southern India.
About how many native speakers: 48 million

## ALLILLANCHU
### (pronounced eye-ee-yaan-choo)

Language: Quechua
Where it's spoken: Throughout the Andes in South America
About how many native speakers: 8 million

## HABARI
### (pronounced ha-BAH-ree)

Language: Swahili
Where it's spoken: The East Coast of Africa
About how many native speakers: 16 million

## HELŌ
### (pronounced hello)

Language: Welsh
Where it's spoken: Wales
About how many native speakers: 874,000

## Nǐ Hǎo
### (pronounced nee haow)

Language: Mandarin Chinese
Where it's spoken: Mandarin Chinese is an official language in five countries, including China, Taiwan, and Singapore.
About how many native speakers: 917 million

## MARHABA
### (pronounced MARR-hah-bah)

Language: Arabic
Where it's spoken: Arabic is an official language in 25 countries, including Chad, Morocco, Iraq, and Libya.
About how many native speakers: 313 million

Kurdistan,
Iraq

# ELISE
# LAUGIER

# REMOTE-SENSING SPECIALIST

A remote-sensing specialist uses a variety of technologies to see entire landscapes from above, as well as what lies beneath the ground.

Elise was just eight years old when she went on her first archaeological dig. Sure, she didn't go to a far-off destination (she was in her family's backyard), nor did she have any special equipment (she dug holes with her shovel), but she did make some exciting discoveries. "I found a couple pieces of broken, painted pottery," she says. "I was thrilled!" After that, it was settled. Elise wanted to become an archaeologist.

And that's just what she did. What Elise loves about her work today is the same thing that excited her about that first dig—discovering clues about what life was like for the people who left them. But there are also some pretty big differences about her work now. For one thing, she's not so close to home any-more. In fact, Elise travels all around the world. And then there's the equipment. It's much, much more high-tech. In recent years, Elise and a growing group of fellow archaeologists have begun using cutting-edge technologies—some of which she helped develop—to help them discover what's buried beneath the ground, from a distance, before they even move a bit of dirt. These tools are called remote-sensing technologies.

"What I love about technology in archaeology, especially satellite remote sensing, is that it offers a big picture, bird's-eye view of entire archaeological landscapes," Elise says. "Technology lets me investigate ancient features that are hidden in landscapes. I am always discovering something new that sheds light on how people lived in the past."

When it was time to choose a location to do her fieldwork, Elise set her sights on one of the most history-rich locations in the world—Mesopotamia. Mesopotamia, which translates to "land between two rivers," is an area in Asia near the Tigris and Euphrates Rivers, in what now includes parts of Syria, Turkey, and Iraq. The first human civilization is thought to have started there around 6000 B.C.

The area's rich soil, stable climate, and access to water made it a fantastic place for farming. During the time that people settled there, a boom in innovation occurred, and what are thought to be the very first cities were developed. Mesopotamians built huge, ornate buildings and temples. They developed math, studied the stars, and even devised the first system for reading and writing.

"When I learned about Mesopotamia, I knew I wanted to go there," Elise says. "It may be the first and the oldest civilization, and it contains the earliest evidence we have in the world for writing, agriculture, and all sorts of things."

For her latest project, Elise has been working in northern Iraq, studying how and where people in Mesopotamia farmed thousands of years ago. Elise and her colleagues have to move fast. People living in the area now aren't always aware of the ancient buildings that are hidden beneath the ground, and as they build new structures, pave new roads, and farm the land, this can hurt and even destroy archaeological sites.

In fact, several times, Elise and her colleagues have arrived to a site, ready to investigate, only to discover it's no longer there and the ground has been dug up and turned into something new. "Once, we got out of the car and went to find a site we'd seen in satellite images, and we were looking around," Elise says, "and we kept looking and looking, and then we realized, it was gone. All the dirt had been moved around, and it was being used to build up a canal for aquaculture [farming]." This makes what Elise does all the more important. "It gives you a sense of urgency, like, 'Wow, we better hurry up and investigate all of these sites before they're gone.'"

To locate artifacts and ruins, Elise and her colleagues first look for places where they suspect there might be some beneath the ground. In Mesopotamia, these areas often look like mounds in the earth, and many times they have little pieces of pottery, called sherds, on the surface. Elise and her team also look for other clues, like the remains of architecture sticking out of the earth, or even places where plants aren't growing as well (because plants don't grow as well on soil that is covering ancient settlements). To find these areas, they study images taken by satellites, which are machines orbiting Earth in space.

"I love satellite imagery because it allows me to explore anywhere in the world right from my computer," Elise says. Then, once the team has scoped out a site, the archaeologists go there in person to get a sense of what the area might have been used for in 4000 B.C.

> **"** The work that I do is documenting our shared human past before it's destroyed by modern human activity. **"**

But that's not the end of the high-tech gadgets. Once on the ground at the location, Elise flies a drone overhead to gather more high-resolution data, like thermal imaging, which can detect changes in plant health and soil moisture that are caused by archaeological features hidden just below the surface. Then, she and her team use ground-penetrating radar, which is like taking an x-ray of the Earth, creating a 3D picture of what the scene belowground might look like.

Finally, when they have a good idea of what they're going to encounter, the team begins to dig. "We're finding so many new things, and they're so well preserved," Elise says. "We're finding whole rooms that are just full of ancient people's stuff."

Elise and her team also create 3D models, using computer software and 3D printers, of everything that they excavate. Since they aren't able to bring artifacts back to the United States with them, these 3D models allow them to study what they've found once back home. It also gives the public a chance to see the cool artifacts they've unearthed!

For Elise, uncovering these treasures isn't just fascinating—it's urgent, too. "The work that I do alongside archaeologists in Iraq is really important because it's documenting our shared human past before it's destroyed by modern human activity," Elise says. "Archaeology is for anyone who cares about where we came from, how we got here, and how people lived in the past."

A DRONE'S-EYE VIEW OF ANCIENT ARCHITECTURE EXCAVATED AT KHANI MASI, KURDISTAN, IRAQ

# INSPIRATION STATION
## Elise's Advice for Aspiring Archaeologists

"Remember: Technology is a tool that helps you answer the questions you're interested in, but the questions have to come from your own interests and your own studies."

## ELISE'S MUST-HAVE

Laptop, GPS, and snacks! On an excavation, Elise's laptop holds all her data, her GPS tells her where she is, and snacks keep her energetic! Her favorite snacks? Trail mix and chocolate bars.

Manila, Philippines

# HANNAH
# REYES MORALES

## VISUAL STORYTELLER

Visual storytellers create photos, videos, or illustrations and put them together to tell real-life stories about people and events.

Hannah Reyes Morales spent most of her childhood close to home. She lived in a neighborhood in Manila, the capital city of the Philippines. Her mother was afraid of the crime around their neighborhood, so, aside from her daily walks to and from school, Hannah stayed in their house to keep safe.

Luckily, behind her house, there was a small, gated courtyard where her family stored things and washed and hung the laundry. The whole area was paved, aside from one tree and a couple of plants. "My best friends were the roots of the tree that grew in the cracks in the asphalt," Hannah says. "Growing up in the center of Manila, I didn't have access to nature. But, in a way, with this little outdoor area, I did. And I got to know that tree and those plants."

Hannah had an active imagination and an endless curiosity about the people and places that existed beyond the walls of her house. "The only window I had to the outside world was photographs," Hannah says. She found a shelf filled with her mother's *National Geographic* and *Life* magazines, and she remembers seeing a photograph of a gorilla touching the famous primatologist Jane Goodall's hair.

Hannah was struck by the fact that, unlike the characters in the Harry Potter books she so loved to read, the people in these pictures—living in such faraway places, doing what seemed like magical things—were real. She realized, too, that without photographs, she would never have known these people existed, or have been able to learn about their lives. It was then that she understood the power photography can have.

> " The only window I had to the outside world was photographs. "

As Hannah got older, her interest in taking photos grew. At first, she took simple, instant photos with a Polaroid camera. She read photography books, learning everything she could about photographers she admired. Then, when she was 18 years old, she received her first proper camera as a gift from her mother, a Canon 400D.

"I think that I wanted to be a photographer because I wanted to travel," Hannah says. "I thought that if I had a camera, it would be like a passport—a way out." It would be a while, though, before Hannah had the means to travel. "I read that if you want to be a photographer, you have to be able to make good images from your own backyard. So I started thinking about how to tell stories from my home."

Hannah began to photograph the woman who cooked for her family and lived with them in her family home, whom they called Nanay. "Nanay raised me, and as a child I always wondered why she was not part of our family photos," she says. "When I started this project, it was just for us. I wanted to have a family history that didn't exclude her."

Hannah's photos of Nanay eventually appeared on a major U.S. newspaper's photography blog, and then other media outlets saw them and published them as well. Even after this exciting success, though, Hannah still needed to work several different jobs—as a web designer, part-time photographer, and clothing seller—and, still, she could barely afford the basic things she needed. But, determined, Hannah continued taking photos and sending them to publications, hoping that one day her photography work could pay the bills and become her full-time job.

Around that time, Hannah began to use her camera to tell more stories about life in the neighborhoods near her home. Many of these neighborhoods were coping with poverty, high crime rates, drugs, and violence. But instead of focusing on that, she decided she would tell stories about "moments of tenderness in the midst of difficult situations."

Hannah frequently took photographs in Tondo, one of the poorest districts in Manila. Here the streets and alleyways are narrow and crowded with people day and night. "It has some of the most beautiful light in the world," Hannah says. "Manila sunsets are the best sunsets."

It was during one such sunset that Hannah met a little girl named Puti. "It was one of those moments that will stand out for me forever," Hannah says. Puti, a talkative, curious little girl, was playing by herself, climbing up and down a tree when she spotted Hannah taking photos. "I showed her some of the photos, and she began chatting with me. She told me her dream was to become a queen and that the dress she was wearing was her favorite. She said, 'It's beautiful when Papa washes it.' Her father, she told me, collected coal for a living. And it made me think a lot about how, at that age, all children have equal dreams, but they don't always have equal opportunities."

Then, something amazing happened. One of the photos Hannah took of Puti was chosen to be featured in a collection for International Women's Day 2018. And the person who chose Hannah's photo was none other than Emma Watson, an activist for women's issues and an actor, famous for her role as Hermione in the *Harry Potter* movies! The photo received a lot of attention. "When I was photographing [Puti], I thought of it as a private moment that would exist only in my heart," Hannah says. "But to have that photo seen by so many, and to have it chosen by Emma Watson, who was my role model growing up—it was a dream come true!"

Since that time, Hannah has found international success as a photographer, and she has had photos published by many top magazines and news organizations. In fact, for recent assignments, she has traveled from her home in the Philippines to Mongolia, Brazil, Nigeria, and South Sudan. While Hannah's childhood dream has certainly come true—she is able to travel and explore other countries, and to connect with many different people across the globe—one lesson she learned early on is that powerful storytelling can be done no matter where you are. "Don't wait to tell stories until you can travel to a very far-off place," she says. "Interesting things are happening to everyone, everywhere, and you can uncover them by asking and being curious."

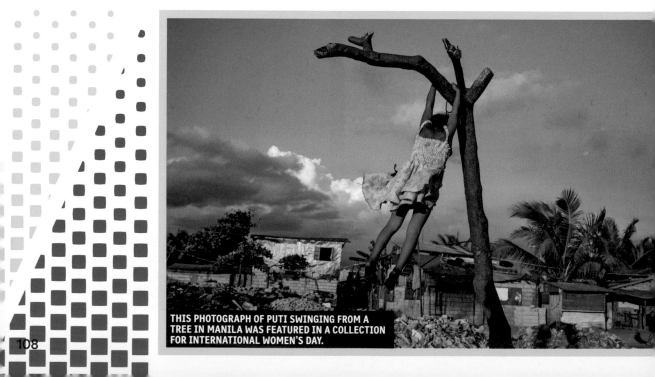

THIS PHOTOGRAPH OF PUTI SWINGING FROM A TREE IN MANILA WAS FEATURED IN A COLLECTION FOR INTERNATIONAL WOMEN'S DAY.

## HANNAH'S READING REC

*Open House for Butterflies* by Ruth Krauss, illustrated by Maurice Sendak. "I'm a huge fan of children's books," Hannah says. "This one has a bunch of quirky illustrations and funny lines like, 'You should make a sad face when you meet a crocodile.' It's just like how I want to see the world—a little bit strange, a little bit whimsical, but always magical."

A MAN PHOTOGRAPHED BY HANNAH IN PHNOM PENH, CAMBODIA

HANNAH'S PHOTOS CAPTURE SCENES OF EVERYDAY LIFE IN THE PHILIPPINES.

## INSPIRATION STATION
### Hannah's Advice for Aspiring Photographers

"For me, it's all about persistence. When I started out, I was told that my photos were just pretty and nothing more. It was discouraging, but I took it as a challenge, and I started learning little by little. I took workshops and viewed more photos until I felt I could really tell the stories I wanted to tell, with my own vision and my own voice. It took persistence, but that persistence paid off."

## HANNAH'S MUST-HAVE

Headphones! When she travels to distant locations to work, Hannah always listens to music. "Music keeps me sane and centered," she says.

HANNAH HAS DOCUMENTED LULLABIES AROUND THE WORLD. IN THIS PHOTO, A MONGOLIAN MOTHER SINGS HER CHILD TO SLEEP.

Manila is the most densely populated city in the entire world, with more than 71,000 people per square kilometer (a little more than a third of a square mile).

# Story of a Photo

**This image of Zamanbol, a young Altai Kazakh eagle huntress, is one of Hannah's favorite photographs.**

"I met Zamanbol during one of my earlier trips to Mongolia," Hannah says. "Seeing her strength, her connection to her culture and to the wild, and her embodiment of heritage really expanded my notions of what being a girl can be. The image shows her practicing a very old tradition from generations past, but when I look at it I am filled with hope for a future that young girls will lead."

How did Hannah capture Zamanbol's strength? Using the three elements of great photography: light, balance, and emotion.

- Light creates drama and draws the viewer's attention to different parts of the scene. Here, the sunlight behind the eagle creates a beautiful halo around its feathers and draws your attention to the action.

- Life isn't perfectly centered, or symmetrical, so a good photo doesn't need to be, either. Here, the quiet sky and land on the right balances the action-ready Zamanbol and her falcon on the left.

- Finally, the photo captures a sense of wonder. A good photograph also makes you feel something, like joy or sorrow. Sometimes images also make us feel curious; they make us want to learn more about the place or person, like Zamanbol.

# KAKANI
# KATIJA

Moss Landing and the Monterey Bay National Marine Sanctuary, California, U.S.A.

## BIOENGINEER

A bioengineer develops new technologies for studying humans, animals, or plants. Bioengineers also observe animals or plants in nature, to learn new ways of designing useful technologies for humans.

Dr. Kakani Katija grew up watching *Star Wars* movies and reruns of *Star Trek* on TV. She dreamed of becoming an astronaut and being part of a team that explored strange new worlds, looking for life on other planets. When she went to college, she studied to become an aerospace engineer, and then began a graduate program in aeronautics. But as she studied, she realized that manned missions to space were few and far between, and while looking for life on other planets was fascinating, the discoveries were rare. That's when she turned her sights to a place teeming with undiscovered, unidentified species—the ocean.

Kakani began thinking more in depth about how to develop the technologies necessary to study ocean organisms that we don't know much about, and that may be difficult to get to. In graduate school, she participated in an underwater scuba trip to study how jellyfish interact with water, and just how exactly they swim. Kakani learned that biologists often watched and photographed jellyfish in tanks, but it was much more difficult to observe the movements of these squishy, translucent creatures in their natural habitat. So she turned her attention to creating a device to help, one that could light up the area around the animal to illuminate its body so scientists could see just how it operates.

Kakani put together a team of engineers and got to work, designing and building an underwater, high-speed instrument, the Self-Contained Underwater Velocimetry Apparatus (SCUVA). It is a tool, about the size of a microwave, that a scuba diver can carry

> **"**
>
> *I just took a step back and thought, Wow, we are the first people seeing this EVER.*
>
> **"**

underwater. It is equipped with a camera and laser that projects a sheet of light into the dark water, making it possible to see gelatinous creatures like jellyfish, as well as the water moving in and around them. Using the camera, her team made important discoveries about how jellyfish move water around while they swim. The project turned out to be eye-opening for Kakani: It showed her that she didn't need to travel to another planet to explore strange new worlds.

In fact, today Kakani helps biologists explore one of the most mysterious parts of the ocean—a region so deep, very little sunlight can reach it—as an engineer for the Monterey Bay Aquarium Research Institute in Moss Landing, California. Halfway between the surface and seafloor, this region is called midwater and is nicknamed the "twilight zone." Scientists estimate that more than half the life-forms in the twilight zone are still unknown, and the ones we do know of, we know very little about. For Kakani, it was the perfect challenge. "The ocean," she says, "really is the next frontier."

Moss Landing sits right at the entrance to a huge underwater canyon that is home to an amazing array of deep-water organisms. It's a marine researcher's dream. Kakani and her team need to travel only a short distance on a ship to test the instruments they are developing in one of the deepest canyons on Earth.

One of the new instruments that Kakani helped develop, the DeepPIV, uses cameras and lights to get a better understanding of how underwater creatures move. Just as the Wright brothers were inspired by birds when they were creating airplanes, Kakani and her colleagues hope to create new technology based on what they learn.

Another high-tech device Kakani uses in her research is called an ROV, or remotely operated vehicle. Getting to the twilight zone is too dangerous for scuba divers, so researchers use a robotic submersible to descend into the murky darkness. From a control room on board the ship, the ROV pilot maneuvers the vehicle into the right position for observations. Then, the DeepPIV lasers light up tiny particles that naturally exist in water. As an animal moves through the area lit by the laser, its motion disturbs these particles, causing them to move as well. A high-speed camera captures the particles' motion, which reveals the way the water moves around and behind the animal as it swims.

Kakani's device was a success—and it was about to be used to make a very exciting discovery. One of her colleagues—Dr. Bruce Robison—had been studying a particularly mysterious creature: the giant larvacean. But he'd been unable to get a good look at it.

"These animals look like tadpoles," Kakani says, "but they do something so strange. They make these really complex mucus structures, which they secrete from an array of cells on their heads. They blow them up, kind of like balloons around themselves, into a house that they can live in." No one knew the actual shape of their mucus houses, and no one knew exactly how they functioned.

So Kakani set out on a research mission with the biologist's team to try to get a better look at the giant larvacean's mucus house. All eyes were glued to the monitors in the control room of the ship. "I remember as our sheet of laser light crossed the animal," Kakani says. "It went into the house and lit everything up. Suddenly you could see the interior chambers. You could see the animal's tail moving, pumping water into the structure. And the biologist—who'd seen a lot in his 30-plus years of doing research—just said, 'Wowwwww!'"

Everyone in the room was abuzz. They all were in awe. "I just took a step back and thought, *Wow, we are the first people seeing this EVER.*"

With the right tools, Kakani says, the possibilities for new discoveries in the ocean's twilight zone are endless. "This zone," she explains, "is one of the most important parts of the ocean." Every single day, small ocean animals—such as krill, little

jellyfish, and tiny fish—move up and down in the ocean. At night, with fewer predators around, they swim up from the twilight zone to the surface, where they feed. Then, as the sun rises, they swim back down to the twilight zone, where they hide out in the dark. Countless billions of these little marine organisms swim anywhere from 500 to 1,600 feet (150–500 m) each way—almost daily! This daily vertical migration is the largest movement of organisms on our planet.

"These migrating animals are the base of the ocean food web, and we simply don't know enough about them yet," she says. Bigger fish eat these fish, so without them, we wouldn't have any of the fish that we like to eat. And most of their lives are lived in a zone we know so little about.

When someone thinks of what an engineer does, they may not imagine Kakani's real-world, hands-on adventures. Kakani says, "Engineering is a lot more than just electronics, or somebody in a basement sitting in front of a computer. The more you are exposed to the different types of engineering and the different problems that engineers work on, the more you'll realize it's really an incredible career to be involved in."

Kakani and her brother were a competitive figure skating pair—and were even chosen as alternates for the U.S. Olympic team!

Larvaceans use their mucus houses to filter their food—tiny particles of dead or drifting plants and animals—from their environment. When their filters get clogged, they shed them and build new ones.

By observing the movements of ocean animals, bioengineers can discover better ways of moving through and exploring the deep ocean. The result? Bioinspired designs for new underwater vehicles!

## STRAIGHT FROM THE SCIENTIST

*What do you think are the most important things kids should know about being an engineer?*

"It's important to understand that engineers are also scientists. Like scientists, engineers are pushing the boundaries of what is known. As a bioengineer, I have to become familiar with the problems that biologists might face. But I need to be even more familiar with the technologies that might have the potential to help address those problems. Today, scientists from all different fields work together to figure out how to answer complicated questions."

# THE DEEP ABYSS

## A Whole New Underwater World

**M**onterey Canyon extends 9,600 feet (2,926 m) below water—deeper than the Grand Canyon. This underwater wonder lies right off the coast of California, deep beneath the waters of the Pacific Ocean.

The canyon formed through a process called turbidity current erosion. Basically, a turbidity current is a heavy downhill flow of water. It is triggered by a big disturbance, like an earthquake or other geological event, and it is sort of like an underwater avalanche. But instead of snow and ice, it carries water and dirt. In the case of Monterey Canyon, these turbidity currents have, over time, caused nearby cracks in Earth's crust to erode, carving out an extremely deep canyon.

In this deep canyon, there are a host of unique—and sometimes bizarre!—creatures swimming about. Should you hop aboard a submarine, here are a few you could see swimming past the porthole.

### Fangtooth Fish

This very fearsome-looking fish has long, sharp, translucent fangs. When a tempting creature swims past, such as a smaller fish or shrimp, the fangtooth fish will open its mouth and suck it inside.

### Polychaete

The polychaete—Greek for "with much hair"—is nick-named the bristle worm. Its bristle-covered legs, or parapodia, can be used for swimming, walking, or scooping up mud, which helps it burrow.

## Pompom Anemone

This pretty sea creature changes shape, flattening itself on the seafloor or puffing up and rolling around like a tumbleweed. But be careful: It has stinging tentacles, which it uses to catch crustaceans and krill.

## Giant Siphonophore

This bioluminescent sea creature can be up to 130 feet (40 m) long—longer than a blue whale. Unlike most animals, the siphonophore's body doesn't grow longer; it instead clones parts of itself, adding new sections—each with a unique bodily function.

## Salp

This tube-shaped, jelly-like animal is clear and travels through the water by sucking in water on one end and then shooting it out the other, propelling it forward.

## Bloodybelly Comb Jelly

This radiant creature has—you guessed it—a blood-red belly. It moves through the water thanks to its vibrating cilia (microscopic hairlike structures) that cover its body.

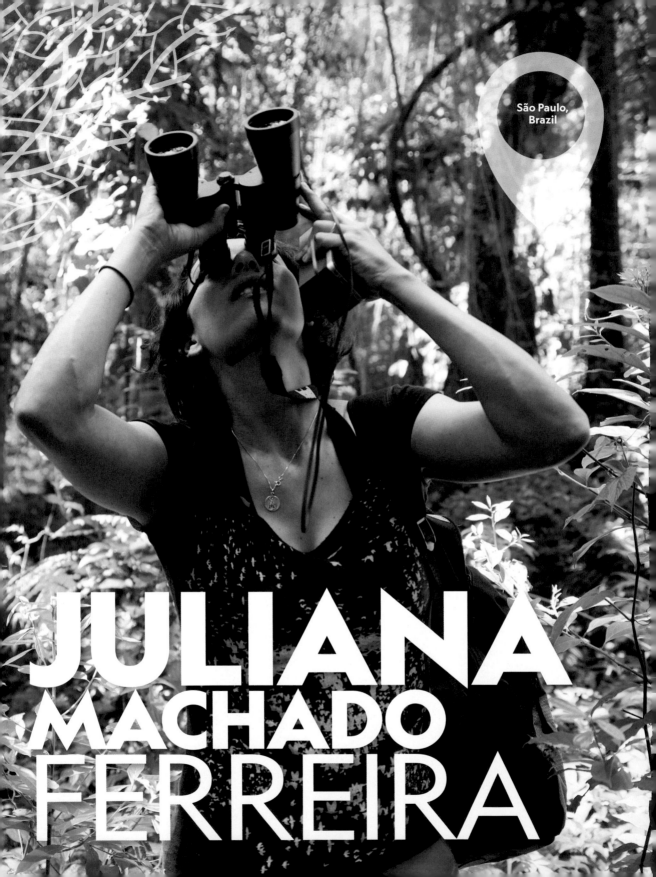

São Paulo,
Brazil

# JULIANA
## MACHADO
# FERREIRA

Someone who uses science to study how to maintain and restore habitats and protect wildlife.

When Dr. Juliana Machado Ferreira was a child growing up in Brazil, her parents kept a songbird as a pet. "My parents were really good people and well informed," she says. "They never thought having songbirds in cages could be a bad thing." But Juliana couldn't help but notice that every time they opened its cage door, the bird was eager to escape. It made her curious, and she began wondering whether it was right to keep an animal confined when it was born to fly.

"I was born with a love for animals and nature," Juliana says. "And my mother says that I've always had a sense of justice." Those two things—her passion for the natural world and her strong convictions about right and wrong—led her to the work she does today fighting animal trafficking in Brazil.

Animal trafficking is an illegal activity in which protected wild animal species are killed or captured and then sold. This includes keeping or selling live wild animals as pets, or selling parts of wild animals—like fur or tusks.

"It's important to understand that wild animal species are different from domestic animal species," Juliana says. "Some animals that are from wild species can be domesticated and kept in a home environment, [but they shouldn't be] because they are still a wild species."

Not only might an individual animal suffer, but the entire ecological system they were taken from could suffer, too. In nature, everything plays a role in the larger system. For example, some animals eat smaller animals, bugs, and plants; some are food for bigger species; and some contribute to their ecosystem by spreading seeds for plants and trees. Removing one part of this delicate cycle can have a big, disruptive ripple effect that can impact other animals and plants, and even human well-being.

In Brazil, there has long been a booming market for wild animals sold as pets, as well as products made with materials from wild animals.

"There's a big cultural habit in Brazil of keeping songbirds in cages so that they will sing," Juliana says. "People think they are beautiful." It's common, too, for people to keep parrots, macaws, iguanas, snakes, monkeys, and other wild animals in captivity. And while there is a legal wild animal breeding industry in Brazil, it fails to meet the incredible demand for wild pets.

Juliana says that she doesn't blame the people who buy the animals as pets. "I'm not judging everyone who owns a wild animal," she says. "Sometimes they don't know better. And I love animals—I want to keep animals in my house as well. But I've just had to learn how to do it, and which ones, and why."

> " My mother says that I've always had a sense of justice. "

A couple of years before starting her Ph.D. in biology, Juliana started volunteering with an organization called SOS Fauna. When the local police find animals that are being trafficked, they seize them from the traffickers. But then they aren't able to care for the animals. SOS Fauna works alongside the police and provides first aid and care to the often hurt and sick animals.

On one of these missions, Juliana first encountered campo orioles, a typically vibrant and strikingly beautiful species of bird. But on that day, they were stuffed in a box, in the trunk of a car, with several other types of birds. "The police were raiding a street market where animals were being sold illegally," Juliana says, "and the officers know that the traffickers keep most of the animals in cars, trucks, or houses nearby. The officer I was working with searched this car, and there they were—all crammed in, with broken beaks and broken legs."

Then, a few months later, Juliana was doing fieldwork with her colleague Fabio Schunck, who is an ornithologist, a kind of scientist who studies birds. It was a cool early morning in northeastern Brazil. "The day was breaking and the sky was all different colors—from purple to pink to blue to yellow—and there were trees all around us," Juliana says. "All these birds were singing, and suddenly in the distance, I heard an oriole. It was the first time I saw one free in nature."

When these orioles are held in captivity, they often aren't able to eat their natural diet, so they turn yellow. But, in the wild, they are a brilliant, bright orange. "I had my camera and I zoomed in on it, and I saw that it was singing from the top of its lungs. It was so incredibly beautiful and free and powerful. That was what that animal was supposed to be doing." Then, she remembered the beautiful birds stuffed in a little box in the back of that car. "That was the moment I knew that I had to keep

trying to help these animals, even if what I was doing was small."

Today, Juliana directs a nonprofit, Freeland Brasil, that works with politicians and lawmakers to help create laws to protect wild animals from trafficking. The team at Freeland Brasil also works to train government agents to combat wildlife trafficking and educate the public, through films and programs in schools, about why it's important not to purchase these wild animals as pets.

"I'm more in a management position right now, rather than in a lab," Juliana says. "Maybe it's not my favorite thing to wear high heels and go to meetings, but it's important work, and it's effective. South America has been getting more attention as an important wildlife trafficking hot spot. We are getting more funding, and governments are paying attention."

Through her work, Juliana has grown to be more open-minded toward people whose opinions and ways of life are different from hers. "I had to learn to really talk with and respect people who think differently from me," she says. "If I could choose, there would be no birds in cages in the world and everybody would be a vegan. But we live in a democracy, and in a free world, and people have different opinions. We need to be able to show our opinions and explain our reasons without judging people and fighting."

Although Juliana started off her career as a researcher, she now wears a lot of different hats in her work—some days she focuses on education, some days she conducts research, and other days she advocates for new environmental policies. But whichever hat she's wearing, she's always focused on her mission to protect the wild animals of Brazil and beyond.

## JULIANA'S READING REC

*Between Two Poles* and *Endless Sea*, both by Amyr Klink. "He's an explorer and a sailor, and I loved all of his books," Juliana says. "Reading has always been a very important part of my life."

JULIANA CONDUCTS FIELDWORK, STUDYING GREEN-WINGED SALTATORS, A TYPE OF SONGBIRD, FOR HER PH.D.

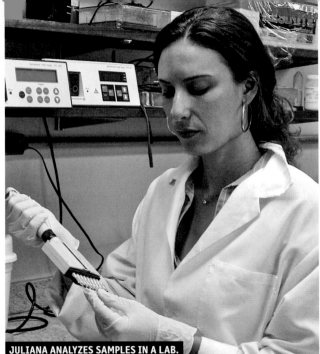

JULIANA ANALYZES SAMPLES IN A LAB.

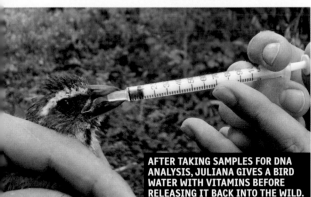

AFTER TAKING SAMPLES FOR DNA ANALYSIS, JULIANA GIVES A BIRD WATER WITH VITAMINS BEFORE RELEASING IT BACK INTO THE WILD.

# INSPIRATION STATION
## Juliana's Advice for Aspiring Conservationists

"If a lot of people are saying no to you—keep on. I think we only change the world if we bother the status quo. We need to change things, and when we change things, people get bothered. They are taken out of their comfort zone. So if you are doing that, keep on going. You are probably doing something right."

## JULIANA'S MUST-HAVE

A machete. When out in the field, it's a useful tool to cut branches or ropes as needed. It also gives her an added sense of security if she were to encounter a dangerous animal or person.

Vatnajökull glacier, Höfn, Iceland

# M JACKSON

Dr. M Jackson had been holding the rope for a climber who was making their way down the side of the Meade Glacier in Alaska, U.S.A., when the climber slipped on some rotten, or mushy, ice. This jerked M's rope, sending her jolting into the air and back down into a water-filled crevasse—a deep crack in the glacier.

Fellow climbers quickly sprang into action, pulling her from the crevasse, and helping her out of her freezing, soaking clothes and into a sleeping bag. The crew couldn't helicopter off the glacier until the next morning, so they spent the night sleeping on the ice. "I couldn't fall asleep," M says, "so I spent a full night, frozen, listening to the sound of the ice cracking and slamming around me. I had never before considered how the ice sounded. I'd never paused—or spent eight hours lying on it—just to listen."

As a glaciologist, M studies natural ice all around the world, including how people interact with and relate to the ice. She examines how people will be impacted by melting ice caused by climate change—the warming of the planet caused by human activities. Certain things that humans do—like burning fossil fuels for electricity, cars, and planes—release greenhouse gases into the atmosphere. These greenhouse gases create a sort of bubble around the planet that traps heat inside, causing it to warm. As Earth continues to heat up, the temperature of the oceans will rise, weather patterns will change, and ice all around the world will continue to melt. M wants to understand the stories of the world's ice, and help tell these stories through her writing.

That night, lying on the ice, listening to the glacier's unique sounds, sinking ever so slightly as her body's heat melted an indentation into the glacier, she had a realization: There were more ways to experience the ice than she'd previously realized.

Through her work studying glaciers, M has embarked on many frigid, physically grueling adventures to explore the ice. While glaciers can be studied in many different ways, including through technology, M likes to get out on the ice in person. "We put lots and lots of gear on—crampons and harnesses, helmets and ropes, ice axes and ice picks, food and emergency equipment," M says, "and we take these very adventurous, physically demanding trips out onto the glacier."

But she also has calmer moments. She's sat down with strangers to learn what it's like for people who grew up around these natural wonders. M has discovered that these quiet moments can be just as valuable as more adventurous ones.

One such experience happened after she had been working in an area called Höfn, in Iceland, for many months, studying the Vatnajökull glacier. She got into a conversation with a local woman about the work that she does. The woman suggested that M accompany her and her sisters to visit the glacier. M was intrigued. In her mind, she thought they would be embarking on another challenging trek. But when the sisters came to pick her up, they had no gear, no equipment.

"I had no idea what we were doing," M says. "We

drive out to this parking lot and we all get out, but instead of going on top of the glacier, we sit in front of the car and just look at it." As they sat there, gazing out at this glacier, the women started telling M about their childhoods living near it. "One of them told me this story about how growing up there she'd always known that glaciers 'bloom,' or that they change color throughout the year." The woman walked M through the glacier's yearly evolution, explaining that in the fall, glaciers are washed by all the rain, leaving them a radiant blue color. Then in winter, all that rain freezes and acts as a mirror, reflecting the sky, making the glacier even bluer. Then, when it begins to snow, the glacier turns white. When spring arrives, the snow starts to wash away, and dust from Iceland's black-sand beaches is blown around, turning the glaciers darker. In the summer, the white and brown parts of the glaciers are exposed to solar radiation and turn a dingy, muddy color. Then fall comes again, and the glaciers are washed and are back to being blue.

M's more human approach to studying glaciers is cutting edge in her field, and it's helping researchers better understand how humans, especially women, interact with these icy wonders. Listening to the women talk about what they knew, as neighbors of this glacier, was a moving experience for M. "I sat there at the end of that day, and I realized that it was one of the most authentic adventures and experiences I've ever had with glaciers. It wasn't out walking on and dominating the ice, but rather just being with somebody who has lived with ice her whole life and listening to how she sees it and how she understands it. It was really profound for me."

M grew up in rural parts of Washington and Alaska. "I grew up in the middle of nowhere," she says. "That meant I got to spend a lot of time outside exploring." But it also meant that there wasn't a lot of opportunity for her to learn about different people, ideas, and areas of study. Even though there are thought to be more than 100,000 glaciers in Alaska, as a young woman M never met a scientist, let alone a female scientist. She didn't know that a career in

> **"**
> What I was passionate about was traveling and being outside, but I didn't have any money and I couldn't go anywhere.
> **"**

science was even a possibility for her. "When I was young, the career paths that I thought about were really shaped by the people I met. So I thought I was going to maybe be a schoolteacher or a firefighter, or that I could work at the local grocery store."

Because M lived in such a remote location, she qualified for a program that would allow her to go straight to college instead of high school. When she graduated from college, she was in her late teens, and she says she felt totally lost. M had many conversations with her parents around the dinner table, trying to figure out what her next step would be.

"What I was passionate about was traveling and being outside," M says. "But I didn't have any money and I couldn't go anywhere." Her dad encouraged her to find a way to see the world if that's what she wanted to do. "You have a great work ethic," he said, "so if you want to travel, just go places and work."

Over the next few years, M traveled around the world, finding whatever jobs she could. "It sounds really glamorous," she says. "But I pulled chickens out of cages, I weeded farms, I taught English—I did anything I could. It wasn't a career, but it was a way to see the world and travel when I had no money to be able to do that." Among those many different experiences, M became a backcountry guide, and some of the terrain that she and the groups passed through contained glaciers. M loved having all these different experiences, and as she did, she began to home in on what it was that she was curious about, what it was she loved. And that, she realized, was science—more specifically, working with glaciers. "The thing that really changed the direction of my career was my very first job with National Geographic as a trip leader and science expert on one of their guided trips to Alaska," she says. "Before then, I'd never thought about glaciers as a career choice. But then I got to interact with people I'd only ever read about in the magazine. I told them what I was interested in, and the response I got back from them was, 'Keep going, keep doing that. If you're interested in that thing, then go for it.'"

And that's exactly what she did.

## HOW TO WALK ON A GLACIER

**STEP 1:** To walk safely on a glacier, you need crampons, which are a type of shoe with metal spikes coming out of the bottom. These spikes keep you planted and safe from slipping up or down the ice.

**STEP 2:** Glacier surfaces are really diverse, and they're often covered with snow or sediments like dirt and similar material. The surface is really uneven—you have to constantly maneuver around many rips and tears in the surface ice—so you have to pay attention. There are a lot of places that are dangerous.

**STEP 3:** You have to listen. The ice pops and it cracks and it makes all these different sounds. There's always water running through it, and you have to pay attention to the sounds because they tell you different things about the ice, like where there might be a hole or where there might be thin ice that you could fall through. It's a really sensory experience to walk on the ice.

## INSPIRATION STATION
### M's Advice for Aspiring Female Glaciologists

"I say, come on! There's so much room for you in this field. It's so new, and it's shaping itself. We need as many diverse perspectives as possible. It is not easy, so the advice I would give is to persevere. Everyone's going to give you excuses for why you don't belong in a space. But if you're passionate about it, just move forward. And build yourself a community of people who support you unconditionally."

### M'S READING REC

*The Only Kayak* by Kim Heacox. "That was the first time it occurred to me that you could go out and make your own community, your own world," M says. "That was a huge book for me when I was younger."

# COOL AS ICE
## The Anatomy of a Glacier

Glaciers—slow-moving rivers of ice—form over hundreds of years, when more snow falls than melts, and over time the snow continues to accumulate and then compress into large, thick masses of ice. About 10 percent of Earth's surface is covered by glaciers, and there's more to these icy marvels than first meets the eye! Take a look.

### Equilibrium Line

The line between the accumulation zone and the ablation zone, where the amount of snow being gathered is equal to the amount that is melting.

## Accumulation Zone

Where a glacier grows by gathering new snow and ice. When it becomes too heavy, it begins to flow.

## Moraine

Deposited rocks and dirt left by a moving glacier that had originally fallen onto the glacier or been picked up by it as it moved.

## Terminus

Where the glacier ends and the neighboring land begins.

## Crevasse

A deep crack in the glacier that forms from stress as the glacier moves over rocky terrain.

## Ablation Zone

Where the glacier loses mass, or gets smaller, for various reasons, including melting, evaporation, and avalanches.

# JENNY ADLER

## CONSERVATION PHOTOGRAPHER AND CAVE DIVER

A conservation photographer is someone who takes photographs as part of an effort to preserve, protect, and restore natural resources. A cave diver is someone who scuba dives in underwater caves.

Gainesville, Florida, U.S.A.

On a bright, sunny day in Gainesville, Florida, under a deep blue sky, Dr. Jenny Adler walks into the water wearing her wet suit, with her camera and scuba gear. As she descends deeper, she can feel her mind and body begin to relax. When she dips her head under and gets a glimpse of the crystal clear freshwater spring, she smiles. A school of bluegills swims in front of her mask, a slow-moving manatee floats in the distance, and a little loggerhead musk turtle gracefully glides through the long, flowing, green grass at the bottom of the spring. Ahhhh. Ever since Jenny was a little girl with a pink snorkeling mask, growing up in Massachusetts, U.S.A., her happy place has always been in the water.

Jenny studied marine biology in college and later enrolled in a Ph.D. program in Florida to study the ecology of freshwater snails. When she moved to Florida, she started exploring local freshwater springs on the weekends, and around the same time, she began getting into photography. When she came back from a dive, she would share her images with friends and with her followers on social media. People loved her images—and they had lots of questions! She realized that many local residents did not know much about the ecology of the springs

129

and their significance to Floridians. "I thought, *Wow! Photography has the ability to influence people ... and also to help communicate science,*" Jenny says.

Jenny wanted to use her science background, love of writing, scuba diving prowess, and photography skills to communicate to people the amazing discoveries she was making, and better yet, to show them. So she made the difficult decision to change the focus of her Ph.D. program. Instead of studying snails, she charted her own course, studying environmental education and freshwater conservation. She went on to complete her Ph.D. in Interdisciplinary Ecology and now works as a photographer and science communicator—her dream job.

Ninety percent of Floridians get their drinking water from the huge Floridan aquifer. It lies beneath the ground and stretches the whole length of the state and up into Alabama, Georgia, Mississippi, and South Carolina. The aquifer is made of porous, Swiss-cheese-like limestone, which holds massive amounts of water. There are places where the water can reach the surface, and in these places, freshwater springs form. People can actually swim in them! There are more than 1,000 springs throughout Florida. And because Jenny has a special cave diving certification, she is able to scuba dive down through the springs and into some of the tunnels in the limestone aquifer.

> **" Photography has the ability to influence people and also to help communicate science. "**

The photographs that Jenny takes on these adventures show people that beneath their feet there is a whole other world that is worth learning about and protecting. "The more I talked to people, the more I realized that very few people understood this water and how we're connected to it," Jenny says. "When I photograph these places, my goal is to show them to people in a way that they've never seen them before."

To get to the aquifer, Jenny dives to the bottom of a spring and then swims through a hole, called the spring vent, that leads to the limestone caves. Some of the caves are wide and easy to navigate, while others are narrower—with a strong current that tries to push her out. In these tunnels, Jenny has to use her strength, grab hold of the rocks, and pull herself through.

"The coolest part, I think, of being in the caves is not necessarily what you see," Jenny says. "It's what you feel and what you hear." It's completely silent in the caves, but when Jenny breathes in through her scuba hose, it makes a deep vibration and a noise like Darth Vader in *Star Wars.* "It's actually really meditative. When you exhale, you can feel the bubbles first move up your face, then up your ears, and finally up to the ceiling of the cave. Then the bubbles travel up through the holes in the porous limestone, and as they make their way out the other side—*boom!* You can feel it, a single bubble emerging from the other side of the limestone makes a rumble like thunder."

## INSPIRATION STATION
### Jenny's Advice for Aspiring Adventurers

"Don't let the fact that you don't see someone who looks like you in a certain job dissuade you. Also, there are jobs out there that you might not know about yet. So don't let that discourage you from going after what you're interested in. Do the things you're passionate about, and you just might be able to make that into a career."

Jenny spends a lot of time in the springs and aquifer photographing what she sees. "I've been photographing one spring, called Blue Spring, for six years," she says, "and every time I jump in it's different."

In fact, Jenny had been doing a long-term photo project on the springs, photographing them several times a month, when one day she jumped in and was shocked by what she saw. All the grass was gone. It was unclear why the grass had disappeared, but soon scientists began asking her for her photos to document what had happened. "I didn't mean to," she says. "But I ended up having these photos that are a historical documentation of the ecological decline at this spring."

There are two types of grass found in the springs, springtape and eelgrass, and they're very important parts of the ecosystem. Snails live on the grass, and little turtles hide in it. Also, both turtles and manatees eat the grass. In fact, one species of turtle, the river cooter, needs the grass to survive. Jenny hopes that by telling the story of the springs through the turtles, she will help people care a little bit more about an ecosystem in peril.

Jenny's career hasn't followed a defined path, or a curriculum you can take in school. Instead, she listened to her passions and curiosity and, through them, created her own dream job. "I'm someone who doesn't like to quit," Jenny says, "but I am really thankful that I gave myself the permission and space to change course and do something I never saw myself doing."

## JENNY'S MUST-HAVE

A thermos of hot tea and a sweatshirt! "In Florida, I can actually hop in my car and drive to the springs," Jenny says. "From my driveway I could be at six to 10 different springs within 30 to 45 minutes. Even when it's 100 degrees [38°C] outside, after I've been in 72-degree [22°C] water for several hours—I'm freezing. My lips are blue. I'm shaking. People sometimes look at me crazy when I come out, put on my sweatshirt, and start drinking hot tea—and they're in their bikinis."

## STRAIGHT FROM THE SCIENTIST
### Is cave diving scary?

"I think having a healthy level of fear is really important. That fear helps you run through scenarios in your mind: *If this were to go wrong, what would I do?* The reason I feel safe cave diving is because I've had proper training, and in any situation, I have a plan for what I would do instead of panic. You always have backup lights, you always have backup reels and spools, and you always dive with a buddy, who also has two tanks of air. The two things you can't skip when learning to dive—and in most things that you're really passionate about becoming good at—are time and effort."

# UNDERWATER WORLD

## A Peek Into Florida's Freshwater Springs

When Jenny dives into the water, she's in good company: Florida's freshwater springs have loads of native plant and animal species, all in one place. Here are some of the cool creatures you might find swimming in their crystal clear waters.

### AMERICAN ALLIGATOR

This prehistoric creature can grow to be a giant. In fact, males can reach up to 1,000 pounds (454 kg)! Its rounded snout with upturned nostrils allows it to lie under the water, hidden from view, while still being able to breathe. Fun fact: Its front feet have five toes while its back feet only have four.

### RIVER OTTER

River otters are happy and comfortable both on land and in the water. They have webbed feet, water-repellent fur, and nostrils and ears that close underwater. They breathe air but can hold their breath for up to eight minutes, and they have a third eyelid that allows them to see underwater.

## GREAT BLUE HERON

These beautiful big birds are the largest herons in North America. They grow to be 4.5 feet (1.4 m) tall, with a wingspan of 6.6 feet (2 m). The bird hunts by wading in shallow waters and standing completely still until a fish swims by, then *bam!* The great blue heron pierces the fish with its sharp bill and swallows the fish whole.

## FLORIDA GAR

Native Americans once used the scales of these long, narrow fish as arrowheads. The eggs that the females secrete are poisonous to warm-blooded mammals, and their newly hatched young have a sticky disk-shaped organ on the end of their snout that keeps them attached to aquatic vegetation until they grow to be three-fourths of an inch (2 cm) long.

## FLORIDA MANATEE

These large, gentle giants are nick-named sea cows because they love chomping on seagrass and other aquatic plants. Even though a manatee can weigh up to 1,300 pounds (590 kg), this mammal is a graceful swimmer, using its tail to move forward and its side flippers to steer.

# SARAH STEWART JOHNSON

Kerlingarfjöll, Iceland

## PLANETARY SCIENTIST

Planetary scientists conduct research and experiments to scientifically study planets and other celestial objects in space.

**D**r. Sarah Stewart Johnson spends her days looking for life beyond Earth. "I look for these things called 'biosignatures,' which are traces of life," Sarah says, "and some of the most exciting places that we look for biosignatures are in our own solar system." She and her fellow scientists use biology and chemistry to look for evidence of living things out in space, like on Mars, or on the moons of Jupiter and Saturn. But to do that, Sarah also spends a lot time testing her life-seeking methods in the most extreme, otherworldly environments on our own planet. That means she has to travel a lot for her science.

Sarah wasn't always interested in science. In fact, when she was little and growing up in Kentucky, U.S.A., her dad used to have to drag her and her sister out to examine things in nature. He would drive them out to nearby roadcuts—hills or mountains that have been cut through to make thruways—to look at the different layers in the rock. He also loved to look at the moon and stars, and he was always willing to share his binoculars, eager to point out things in the night sky to his daughters.

"I was sort of primed to be interested in these subjects," Sarah says, "Even though, when I was about 12 years old, I thought he was boring and that these sorts of things were not what I wanted to do." Sarah enjoyed writing and playing with toy ponies. She envisioned herself being an author—and perhaps even a mom—one day.

But when Sarah got to college, she quickly realized rocks and space were exactly the sorts of things she wanted to learn more about. What's more: She found a way to investigate both at the same time.

Her freshman year, Sarah had a professor who was a planetary geologist—someone who studies the rocks, dirt, and land on bodies in space, such as moons, planets, and comets. And Sarah got the very exciting opportunity to work with him in the lab on an early model for a real Mars rover. Mars rovers are robotic vehicles that are sent into space and placed on the surface of Mars to explore and investigate. Two of NASA's rovers, named Spirit and Opportunity, spent years surveying the dry, rocky surface, all while sending back pictures and data to eager scientists and citizens of Earth.

As Sarah worked on new and different projects with this professor, some of them required that she travel. "I had barely been anywhere my entire life," Sarah says. "But then we went out to the Mojave Desert in California and to a volcano in Hawaii, and it's like the whole world opened up."

Going to new places and seeing different landscapes took her interest in exploration to a whole new level. She was eager to find out more about whether life existed beyond Earth. And since no one had the answers to her questions yet, she set out to find them herself.

One of the places that Sarah studies is Mars. But studying Mars is tricky, because humans can't just hop over there to poke around. While Mars is the second closest planet to Earth, it still would take about nine months for astronauts to arrive there—and they'd have to spend a year and a half on the planet's surface before coming home, waiting for Earth and Mars to come back together on the same side of the sun. Then there's the very serious problem of the high levels of radiation that astronauts would be exposed to on Mars and during the journey there. Radiation, in large doses, isn't healthy for humans.

Earthlings at NASA determined that they can study Mars by sending the Mars rovers there. The rovers could explore, send back photos and videos, and collect information with their scientific instruments. But to develop the instruments that will work in such a foreign, faraway place, Sarah and her colleagues travel to places on Earth with similar physical conditions—such as Antarctica, Iceland, and the Atacama Desert. "We want to practice everything before we actually do it on Mars," Sarah says. "Mars is millions of miles away. So we want to make sure that we develop the right kinds of instruments, tools, technologies, and techniques before we send them there."

A few years ago, Sarah and a group of students were all set to travel to Iceland to try out a new technology called a MinION. It would allow scientists to sequence DNA and RNA on Mars, remotely, in real time. Right before their trip, though, there was one small hiccup—the person who was going to take care of Sarah's son canceled. She contemplated backing out of the trip, but then she had a braver idea—she decided to take her five-year-old son with her. Just as her dad had done with her, Sarah was going to show Henry firsthand what it looked like to ask scientific questions and investigate the answers.

Once in Iceland, Sarah and her team had an arduous journey ahead of them to get to their testing location, Kerlingarfjöll. Sarah drove a big pickup truck—with her son in his booster seat in the back—up steep, unpaved dirt roads, slowly and carefully crossing streams, so that they didn't flood the engine. But when they arrived and took in the red, mountainous landscape, it was all worth it. "Those mountains are just ... they're utterly Mars-like," Sarah says. "And much like Mars, the landscape in Iceland has been shaped by the interaction of glaciers and volcanoes. It's all red and white, and it looks like what some parts of early Mars might have looked like."

From the little mountain huts where Sarah and the students stayed at night, they would trudge out into the bitter cold, with big boots, hiking poles, and puffy jackets, climbing up, up, up the mountains, alongside steep precipices, and past roiling, gurgling hot springs to set up their site. There, they would spread out their gear and begin collecting samples to test with the MinION.

Her son would help the students, marking and taking pictures of all the samples. At night, he and Sarah snuggled together, face to face, in their tiny, freezing hut. "He was such a trooper, and he was so excited," Sarah says. "He'd say, 'I'm a scientist, Mama! We're doing research!'"

The trip was a huge success, and Sarah knew then that being a mom didn't mean she could no longer express the more adventurous parts of herself. "You just have to go for it!" Sarah says. "I think there is room in life to be your full self." Sarah is a scientist and a mom, and, in 2020, her childhood dream of becoming an author also came true. Her book is a true account of all the people in human history to have contributed to the adventurous search for life on Mars, including her own story and discoveries. Her son even appears briefly in the book. "He's really proud to be in this book about Mars. And I'm proud, too!"

> 66
> You just have to go for it! I think there is room in life to be your full self.
> 99

IN ICELAND, STEAM FROM INSIDE THE EARTH IS RELEASED RIGHT NEXT TO GIANT GLACIERS.

## SARAH'S READING REC

*Pilgrim at Tinker Creek* by Annie Dillard. "It's one of my very favorite books," Sarah says. "It's full of astonishing discoveries the author made in her own backyard."

SARAH'S SON ACCOMPANIED HER DURING HER RESEARCH IN CHILLY ICELAND.

# INSPIRATION STATION
## Sarah's Advice for Aspiring Planetary Scientists

"It's not just astronauts who work on questions about space, the moon, and planets like Mars. There are many ways to contribute to space exploration, like conducting lab experiments, guiding robotic explorers, and making observations with telescopes. Lots of computer science challenges need to be solved, and all kinds of new technologies need to be created. But when people pull together, they can do seemingly impossible things!"

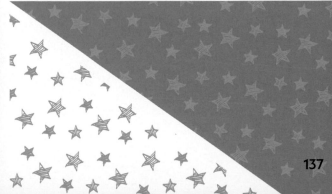

# Dream Team
## Spirit and Opportunity's High-Tech Tools

**ALPHA PARTICLE X-RAY SPECTROMETER**

This tool was used to determine the chemistry of rocks and soils by exposing them to two different kinds of radiation—x-rays and alpha particles—and seeing how the samples reacted.

**MÖSSBAUER SPECTROMETER**

This tool studied rock, soil, and dust samples to determine the composition of the minerals in the samples, and the amount of iron they contained.

**ROCK ABRASION TOOL**

A grinding wheel on this tool could expose fresh rock if scientists wanted a closer look at what was underneath a dusty rock surface that had been worn down by the elements.

In January 2004, NASA landed two rovers on Mars, named Spirit and Opportunity. Their mission? To spend 90 days on the surface of the planet, sending photos and data back to Earth. But these sturdy bots went above and beyond: Spirit worked for nearly six years, and Opportunity lasted more than 14, sending its last transmission in 2018 during a dust storm.

Using data from the rovers, scientists wanted to determine whether there had ever been water on Mars and if the conditions had ever been right for life to have existed. The two rovers landed on opposite sides of the planet, where they explored craters NASA scientists suspected held evidence of water.

The mission proved to be a huge success—both Spirit and Opportunity found evidence of a Martian past with warm and watery conditions potentially hospitable to life. Check out some of the other trusty tools the rovers used to make their groundbreaking discoveries.

## MINIATURE THERMAL EMISSION SPECTROMETER

Nicknamed the Mini-TES, this piece of equipment detected the patterns of thermal radiation of rocks and soils. This information helps scientists determine what minerals make up the rocks and soils that were tested.

## MAGNETS

Different types and strengths of magnets were put on the rovers to attract any magnetic dust particles. These grains would then be examined further to determine whether they held any clues that may point to a watery past.

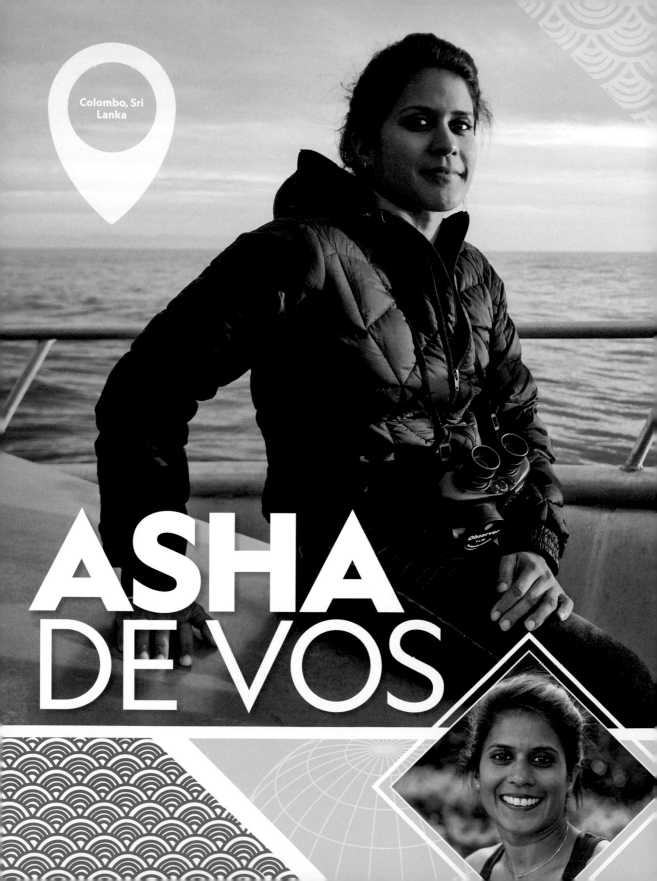

# ASHA
# DE VOS

MARINE BIOLOGIST

A marine biologist is a scientist who studies living things in the world's oceans and other saltwater habitats.

**A**s a little girl growing up in Sri Lanka, Dr. Asha de Vos would spend hours lying on the floor of the National Museum in Colombo, staring up at the blue whale skeleton that hung from the ceiling. It was a 65-foot (20-m) giant—as long as a semi-truck. Asha wondered what this mysterious animal must look like, with all the flesh on its bones, swimming through the vast ocean. Even though her country was surrounded by the sea, she had never seen a living whale.

Although Sri Lanka is a tropical island, Asha says that her family didn't go to the ocean very often. "Nobody in my family really has any interest in water in the same way I do," she says. "But I was brought up in a family that encouraged curiosity." That encouragement led Asha to the pages of adventure magazines, marveling at photographs of ocean explorers. She wanted to know more about the mysteries that lie underneath the dark water. "I wanted to see things no one else could see," she says. "And I wanted to go places no one else would ever go."

When Asha decided to major in marine biology in college, her parents supported her choice, even though it was an area of study they weren't really familiar with. It was a leap of faith on their part, and for everyone she knew. Before Asha became a marine biologist, no one from Sri Lanka had ever received a Ph.D. in marine mammal research. There were no marine biology programs in Sri Lanka, so Asha went to a university in Scotland, where she specialized in marine mammals. Asha was definitely nervous, but she was also very excited.

"I was moving away from home for the first time in my life, and I wasn't just moving down the road," Asha says. "I was moving across the world to a whole new culture, climate, and community. I wasn't sure what to expect, but I was ready for the adventure and the opportunity it would bring."

After college, to get some experience in the field, she volunteered with a number of marine research and conservation projects in New Zealand. While there, one of her professors in Scotland wrote to tell her about an amazing whale research vessel that had just set out on a five-year journey around the globe, to study the effects of ocean pollution on sperm whales. Within the year, the researchers planned to sail near Sri Lanka and the Maldives, a group of smaller islands to the south.

Asha couldn't believe it: A research vessel ... studying whales ... so close to her home? Her mind filled with possibilities. She wanted to be on that ship more than anything! But how could she make that happen? This was before smartphones and the internet were everywhere. But she was determined to get a message to the owner of the boat. So she gathered up what little money she had and headed to the nearest internet café.

"I'd like to get on board," she wrote him, "and I'm the only Sri Lankan who's ever wanted to do this." The next day she went back to the café, to see if he'd written back. He had! Asha was so excited. She opened the email and read: "Thank you for contacting us. We don't have an opportunity for you."

Asha felt defeated, but she didn't give up. She went back to the café the next day and the next and the next. "I wrote to the owner every day for three months," she says. She told him more about herself and about her interests and aspirations. She told him she just wanted to learn more about whale research and how it's done. Her persistence paid off. The boat's owner said she could join them on board for two weeks if she was able to get to the Maldives in one day. Asha quickly packed her things and hopped on the next available flight. "I turned up there 24 hours later," Asha remembers. "I think I shocked everyone!"

Asha was hired as a deckhand. "I was cleaning toilets and polishing brass," she says. "But that didn't bother me, because once I got there, I knew I could prove to them I could do the science, too."

And she did. After just two weeks, the team invited Asha to join them for the research leg of their journey in Sri Lanka as a science intern. One beautiful, flat, calm day on the water, it was Asha's turn to look out for sperm whales in the area. Asha really wanted to be the one who spotted a whale. She could imagine herself getting to call out to the rest of the crew, "Sperm whale!" But hours went by, and she didn't spot a single one. Asha was disappointed as her watch was nearing its end. Then, suddenly, she saw a huge blow in the distance. "All sperm whales have one nostril on the left side, so when they exhale, it's easy to recognize their blow," she says. "But what I saw that day was a gigantic, towering blow that went straight up to the sky, and I knew right away it wasn't a sperm whale." Asha called down to the captain to tell him what she was seeing. She said she thought it might be a blue

> **"** Once I got there, I knew I could prove to them I could do the science, too. **"**

whale, and she asked if they could get closer to take a look. To her surprise, the captain took her word for it, turned the vessel around, and gunned it in the direction of the blow.

As they approached, Asha soon realized it wasn't one blue whale, but six! All the textbooks she'd read in college said that blue whales fed in the cold ocean waters near the poles and migrated to warmer waters near the Equator to breed and give birth to their calves. Asha couldn't believe her luck. Here, off the coast of Sri Lanka, she might actually get to see a blue whale calf, or even a calf being born! The scientists waited and watched. But they didn't see any calves. "The whales were just diving down and coming back up, very lazily," Asha says. Not much was happening, but she convinced the captain to hang around just a little longer. Then, 15 or 20 minutes later, a big red patch appeared on the water.

"One of the whales had pooped," Asha says. "I always tell people that my career started with a pile of poop, because, when I saw it, I realized, if they're pooping here, that means they are feeding somewhere very close." As far as she knew, blue whales fed on tiny organisms called krill that live in cold water, but not here, so close to the Equator. Were all the textbooks wrong? What exactly was going on?

That very night, Asha started outlining her first research proposal. She wanted to know more about if and how the whales had adapted to feed in warmer waters. Most people in Sri Lanka had no idea that blue whales lived in these waters. There was no one else from her country who had ever studied them, so she emailed blue whale experts around the world to ask them for advice. It took her five years to save enough money to officially begin her research. Eventually, Asha became the first person to discover that there is a population of blue whales that live their entire lives in the warm waters of the northern Indian Ocean, where Sri Lanka is located. They don't migrate like other blue whales, and instead of krill, they eat tiny shrimp. She observed that they dive deeper than other blue whales, and they stay under longer, to get the food they need. "So, they're not just blue whales, but they are a unique population, well adapted to these particular waters," Asha says. In fact, they are so different from blue whales in other waters that Asha has dubbed them the "Unorthodox Whales."

Like many types of whales across the world, though, these whales are endangered. Being hit by ships and getting tangled in fishing nets are the main threats to their safety. In particular, Asha documented deadly collisions with giant container ships near the busy harbors of Sri Lanka. These collisions still happen, and Asha is determined to find ways to stop them, keeping in mind the important role the shipping industry plays in our lives. "These whales are so special," she says, "we have to make sure we protect them."

A few years after earning her Ph.D., she returned home and founded Oceanswell, Sri Lanka's first marine conservation research and education organization. Through her organization, Asha hopes to help kids (and adults!) from all over the world explore, connect with, and develop a greater understanding of the oceans, and of the whales that live there. Together, she believes, the people of Sri Lanka can help save whales near their home from the dangers they face and in the process, create a cleaner, safer, healthier environment for everyone.

### ASHA'S MUST-HAVE

A camera! It's the one thing she always takes with her in the field.

## INSPIRATION STATION
### Asha's Advice for Aspiring Female Scientists

"I've learned that you have to work hard, so that at some point people no longer see you for your gender or background, but they see you as a necessity, because you're the only person in the room who can solve the problem at hand."

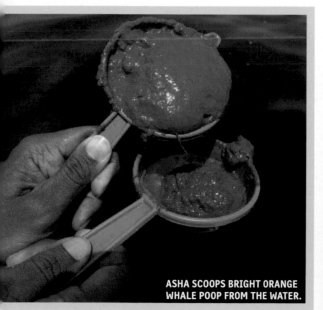

ASHA SCOOPS BRIGHT ORANGE WHALE POOP FROM THE WATER.

# Poop—What Is It Good For?

Typically, when animal poop is spotted, people move away. But not scientists. They often go in for a closer look. And with good reason, too! An animal's poop holds all sorts of information about their life and health. It's also a great way to gather scientific data without having to sedate the animal or draw blood. "People think of poop as this yucky waste product," Asha says, "but to me, poop is like gold! It gives us a look into the animals' lives that we wouldn't be able to get otherwise."

Here are a few things that scientists can learn from an animal's poop:

- Whether they're able to have babies, or if a female is already pregnant.

- If they're healthy or if they're sick. And if they're sick, what it is that's making them sick.

- What they eat. In fact, scientists can do DNA tests to determine exactly what types of animals and plants they were feeding on.

- Their stress levels, by testing the level of stress hormones.

Badgers dig rectangular community toilets in the ground.

Otter dung, called spraint, can sometimes smell like violets.

When goats poop out the fruits they eat from argan trees, locals collect them and harvest the seeds inside to make argan oil, which is used in foods and cosmetics.

An adult African elephant can produce up to 300 pounds (136 kg) of poop a day!

The nitrogen in whale poop has been found to promote the growth of phytoplankton, a plant that removes carbon from the atmosphere, which helps lessen climate change.

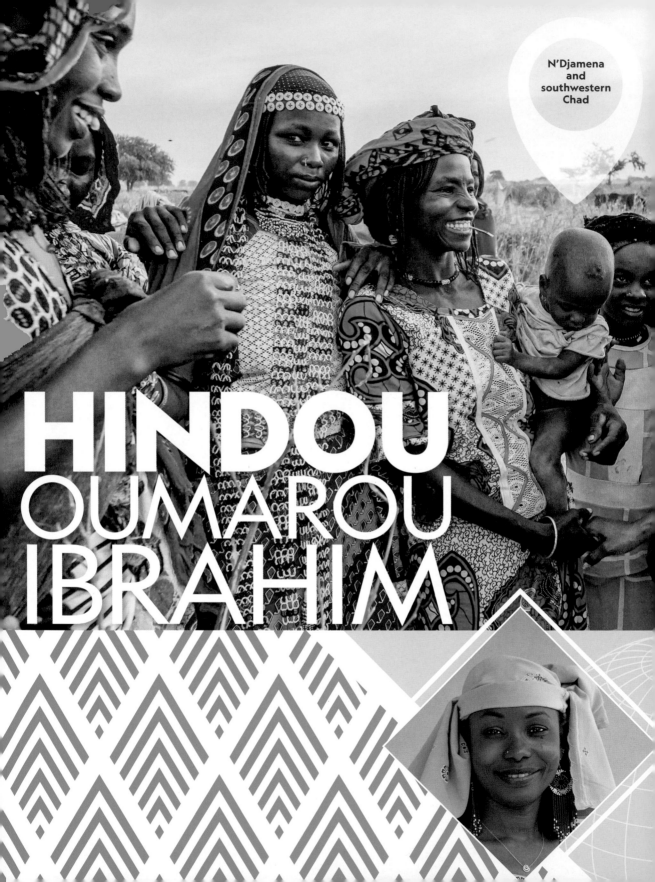

# HINDOU
# OUMAROU
# IBRAHIM

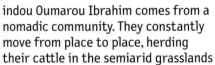

Hindou Oumarou Ibrahim comes from a nomadic community. They constantly move from place to place, herding their cattle in the semiarid grasslands of Chad, a country in Africa. Their cattle provide food and milk for the farmers, who can also trade cattle for other things they need. For countless generations, Hindou's ancestors have survived in this challenging environment. Today, however, Hindou's people are suffering from the consequences of a global problem: climate change.

The nomadic lifestyle has made Hindou and her fellow community members very attuned to the environment and the natural rhythms of nature. But now, years of extreme drought have reduced their cattle herds to a fraction of what they once were, and the cows are making less and less milk. "The rain doesn't come when people expect it to," Hindou says. "The native grasses and other plants our cattle rely on are dying, and new plants are growing that no one even knows the name of. We just call them the 'bad herbs,' because they make the cattle sick."

Hindou's community has been among the first in the world to suffer directly from the effects of climate change, but with limited access to the necessary information, they have also been among the last to find out why these changes are happening. As Hindou has learned more about climate change, she has become an important environmental activist, someone who works to create positive environmental change while educating people from her community about the issue.

"Lake Chad has been a very sad example of the impact of climate change," Hindou says. The lake, which borders Cameroon, Niger, Nigeria, and Chad, is a vital resource for local fishers and farmers, as well as for the cattle herders. "When my mom was young, the lake covered such a large area, and there was plenty of room for people to move around it and use its resources. But by the year 2000, 90 percent of the water had disappeared—it just evaporated—mostly because of climate change."

At the same time, the population in the region surrounding the lake has grown. Since 1960, the population has boomed from five million people to nearly 40 million today. The growing human pressure on a dwindling resource has sparked conflict among the people.

## ENVIRONMENTAL ACTIVIST

An environmental activist speaks up on behalf of endangered ecosystems and inspires people to work together to restore and protect those ecosystems.

Hindou has devoted her life to making sure her community understands exactly what is happening. She also wants to ensure that their voices are heard, and that their traditional ecological knowledge is considered in the discussions that are had as people around the world face the climate crisis.

As Hindou stands up for the people in her community, she is inspired by her own mother, who did what she believed was right, even when others disagreed with her. "I have been so lucky to have my mom as a support and role model," Hindou says. When Hindou was little, girls in her community almost never went to school. But when her mom left their community to start working in N'Djamena, the capital city of Chad, she decided to send her daughters to school, even though her relatives did not approve. While she wanted Hindou and her sister to learn new things and have the sort of education she didn't have, she also wanted them to understand where they came from. Hindou's mom always took Hindou and her sister back to their community for the holidays. They would learn to milk cows, take care of the cattle, and do everything other kids did in a nomadic society.

When she first started school in the city, the city kids looked down on her because she came from a rural area, Hindou says. They would tease her and say she "came from the bush and smelled of milk."

"I couldn't understand it," Hindou says, "but when I started growing up, I realized how lucky I was, and I started to think about all the girls who never get a chance to go to school." And instead of just feeling sad about what those girls were going through, she did something about it. She was just 14 years old when she created an organization to support the rights of girls from rural communities. The organization sought to help them avoid early marriages and get a chance to pursue their own dreams. It was a challenging task for a young girl, but Hindou says it was her mom's strength that inspired her: "I figured that if my mom could stand up and fight the opinions of her whole community to send us to school, maybe I have that same strength, too."

> **"** When I started growing up, I realized how lucky I was, and I started to think about all the girls who never get a chance to go to school. **"**

When Hindou turned 16, she headed to college in the city of N'Djamena and began attending meetings on climate change, sharing information about the effects that she and her community were experiencing in Chad. It was at one of the meetings that an ambassador from Cameroon took notice of her commitment to helping girls and women and invited her to a women's conference in his country. There, she met many people who were working to support indigenous peoples, as worsening droughts and floods, and loss of biodiversity were threatening their way of life. Hindou was invited to even more meetings in New York, U.S.A., and Kenya, and then to the 2015 United Nations Climate Change Conference in Paris, France, where she gave a speech in front of world leaders, climate scientists, and environmental activists. She explained to them how climate change was affecting her people—how women and children are left behind to look after the cattle as their husbands and fathers find jobs in nearby towns and cities just to make ends meet. She was also convinced that there was a lot that the scientists could learn from indigenous peoples, people who are the original inhabitants of a place, that might help them begin to solve the problems caused by climate change.

After the conferences, Hindou wanted to bring back what she'd learned to the people of her community. Traditionally, however, women weren't allowed to take leadership roles like that—especially not young women! Her first step was to try to explain the importance of her message to her community leaders.

"When I sat down with the chief," she says, "I explained to him why their resources were shrinking, and why they couldn't get the help they needed, for better schools and health care." The chief agreed to let Hindou talk to the women of the community, but she still wasn't allowed to meet with the men.

"You are the ones who educate the children and who pass on the traditional knowledge," she told the women. "You need to start making decisions that affect the whole community with the men, because it is also your future." It took several years of trying to convince the men, but finally they let her and the other women join their meetings and have a say in the decisions. She also started to work with both the men and women in her community to document how they'd seen climate change impact their environment.

Today, Hindou travels around the world to help people understand the impact of climate change on her community and on other indigenous peoples. Now that she's found her own voice, she's pushing for other indigenous women to get a seat at the table. She hopes that by involving more women and indigenous communities in global environmental decisions, all the people living in threatened ecosystems will find new ways to work together, to restore and preserve their environment and their way of life.

## WHAT IS TRADITIONAL ECOLOGICAL KNOWLEDGE?

Indigenous peoples are communities that were the original inhabitants of a particular area. They may have been living in a place for hundreds or even thousands of years. Indigenous peoples' knowledge about the plants, animals, water, soil, and weather patterns in their own ecosystems is often passed down from generation to generation. This knowledge is essential for the sustainable use of the resources available to them and for ensuring their long-term survival as a people. Today, as scientists work to understand how climate change is affecting different ecosystems around the world, they survey native communities to collect this "traditional ecological knowledge" (or TEK). This information helps them estimate what environmental conditions were like in the past.

## INSPIRATION STATION
### Hindou's Advice for Aspiring Activists

"I think that first you need to create confidence, trust, and a good relationship between you and the community. You cannot say you want to help your community if you feel you are already above them, or different from them."

# BE A CLIMATE CHAMPION
## HOW TO GREEN YOUR ROUTINE

**Here's what we know:** Scientists have discovered that human activity is causing our planet to warm. This is called climate change, or global warming. Certain gases in Earth's atmosphere trap heat, causing the planet to get hotter. These "greenhouse gases" include carbon dioxide, methane, chlorofluorocarbons, and others, and they are emitted through activities like producing energy, deforestation, and the burning of fossil fuels to power cars, planes, and trains.

**Here's why it matters:** As Earth warms and the climate changes, there are—as there has been and will continue to be—increasing impacts on weather, sea level rise, crops, and more.

**Here's what we can do:** Everyone can do their part to help the planet and limit their contribution to climate change. Here are just a few ways you can be part of the solution.

### Write to your leaders.

Find out who your local leaders are—your mayor, governor, or congressional representatives, for example—and write them a letter (an adult can help you find their office address online). Be honest and polite, and tell them why you care about climate change. Encourage them to support laws that will help the environment.

# Reduce your carbon footprint.

This means reducing the amount of carbon dioxide that is released into the atmosphere because of your activities. Here are a few ways to do this: Suggest that your family walk or ride a bike to nearby destinations instead of driving in a car, use less AC and heat in your home, turn off electronics when you're not using them (or even better, unplug them!), eat less meat, and swap incandescent lightbulbs with energy-efficient compact fluorescent lights.

# Recycle!

Make sure your family and schoolmates are recycling properly. If you notice lots of plastic bottles in trash cans, ask your teachers or other school leaders if you can start an information campaign to make sure everyone knows what can be recycled and the proper way to do it.

# Spread the word.

Start a club at school or in your neighborhood to raise awareness about climate change. Talk to your family, classmates, teammates, teachers, restaurant owners, faith leaders, and political leaders about why you are concerned about climate change and what everyone can do to help.

# Keep learning!

Keep reading, researching, and listening to scientists and experts about climate change and what you can do to help! You can be a powerful force for positive change.

**1** Dominique Gonçalves
Gorongosa National Park,
Mozambique

**2** Wasfia Nazreen
Seven Summits: Everest, Cerro
Aconcagua, Denali, Kilimanjaro,
Elbrus, Mount Vinson, Puncak Jaya

**3** Aubrey Roberts
Svalbard archipelago,
Norway

**4** Patricia Chapple Wright
Ranomafana rainforest,
Madagascar

**5** Nora Shawki
Nile Delta, Egypt

**6** Danielle N. Lee
St. Louis, Missouri, U.S.A.

**7** Jean Beasley
Topsail Island, North Carolina,
U.S.A.

**8** Carolina Freitas
Amazon Basin, Brazil

**9** Munazza Alam
La Serena, Chile

**10** Ella Al-Shamahi
Socotra, Yemen

**11** Stephanie Grocke
Santa María Volcano,
Quetzaltenango, Guatemala

**12** Annie Griffiths
Baffin Island, Canada

**13** Moreangels Mbizah
Hwange National Park,
Zimbabwe

**14** Jennifer Pharr Davis
Appalachian Trail, U.S.A.

**15** Mallory Dimmitt
Florida Wildlife Corridor, U.S.A.

ARCTIC

NORTH
AMERICA

ATLANTIC
OCEAN

SOUTH
AMERICA

PACIFIC
OCEAN

OCEAN

EUROPE

ASIA

AFRICA

INDIAN
OCEAN

AUSTRALIA

ANTARCTICA

# INDEX

**Boldface** indicates illustrations.

# INDEX

# PHOTO CREDITS